Case Studies in Managing School Library Media Centers

by
Daniel Callison
and Jacqueline Morris

ORYX PRESS
1989

The rare Arabian Oryx is believed to have inspired the myth of the unicorn. This desert antelope became virtually extinct in the early 1960s. At that time several groups of international conservationists arranged to have 9 animals sent to the Phoenix Zoo to be the nucleus of a captive breeding herd. Today the Oryx population is nearly 800, and over 400 have been returned to reserves in the Middle East.

Copyright © 1989 by
The Oryx Press
2214 North Central at Encanto
Phoenix, AZ 85004-1483

Published simultaneously in Canada

Printed and Bound in the United States of America

Library of Congress Cataloging-in-Publication Data

Callison, Daniel, 1948–
    Case studies in managing school library media
centers.
    Bibliography: p.
    Includes index.
    1. School libraries—Administration—Case studies.
2. Media programs (Education)—Management—Case studies.
I. Morris, Jacqueline. II. Title.
Z675.S3C182   1989   025.1′978223   89-3360
    ISBN 0-89774-441-1

To Marjorie Sullivan.

She quoted Jerome Bruner's philosophy in her lectures and in her writings. The major theme I remember most was that "the teacher must be not only a communicator, but a model learner, competent, and enthusiastic." Marjorie was letting us know that this was the most important role of the school library media specialist long before the goals and objectives of the new national guidelines were written. I am thankful that she has been my model for learning, for raising questions, for not giving up hope that our field will continue to grow professionally. I am thankful for her friendship. *(DC)*

To Ferne S. Johnson, mentor and friend who periodically, when the need is great, helps me rediscover the vision. *(JM)*

DANIEL CALLISON

Assistant Professor and Associate Dean for the School of Library and Information Science, Indiana University, Bloomington, Daniel Callison has experienced many of the management problems discussed in this book while serving as a director for media programs at Topeka (KS) High School from 1973 to 1979. This inner-city school housed a statewide demonstration media facility from 1976–78. Callison is currently a member of the Editorial Board for the AASL journal *School Library Media Quarterly.*

JACQUELINE MORRIS

President of the American Association of School Librarians 1988–89, Jacqueline Morris is Manager of the Learning Resources Unit, Indiana Department of Education, and serves as an adjunct faculty member for the School of Library and Information Science at Indiana University, Indianapolis. Morris has worked as a building-level school library media specialist in Georgia, North Carolina, and Indiana. She was supervisor for elementary and secondary media programs for the Fort Wayne (IN) Community Schools. She is the Associate Editor for *Indiana Media Journal.*

Contents

Preface

Since 1981, Daniel Callison and Jacqueline Morris have shared teaching responsibilities for a course in school library management. One approach used on both the Bloomington and the Indianapolis campuses has been to establish a management problem through the use of scenarios or case studies for which the student must research the literature and finally present a solution. This is a common approach in other management courses, and the technique often allows for a great deal of discussion, as well as leading to other issues related to the overall operation of a modern school media program.

In the early 1980s, the available case studies for school media centers were outdated. As new cases were suggested in class, and formalized as written case studies, the idea to take the cases to the practicing librarian for reaction was considered. No other publication of management case studies had made the effort to (1) validate the problem as one that is currently of major importance in the field, and (2) seek responses from those who encounter such problems on the front line. In gathering responses from the field and from graduate students, it was discovered that as much valuable discussion came from debating the aspects of a person's response as the issue posed by the case itself. Thus, this publication of case studies provides library science students and library/media center managers with tested scenarios from which they can gain ideas from the experiences of others, and gain leads to more expertise through the literature. Annotated bibliographies are given for the cases in this collection.

In order to identify those problem areas that pose the most important issues to school library management, the editors of the publication sketched 68 possible situational problems. These usually involved only a few lines of description, but directly and clearly raised the problem. The editors gained leads from most of the directors of state media services in order to identify qualified practicing school librarians nationwide who might react to the posed problems. Over 200 practicing librarians on the elementary school and secondary school level were contacted. Each was asked to react to the 68 problems by rating those problems that they felt were of major importance. This process narrowed the list to 36, and three additional situations were added, based on suggestions received from reviewers.

The editors expanded each of the 39 situational problems into case studies. The practicing librarians who reviewed the original 68 situational problems also indicated which, if any, of the problems they would be willing to respond to at length. Expanded scenarios were matched to school librarians, educators, and some state department consultants who wanted the chance to respond. The result, after a year of correspondence, is publication of *Case Studies in Managing School Library Media Centers.* Thirty-two of the scenarios survived as those that represent important management problems facing the modern school library media specialist. Review of these 32 case studies, the responses, and the related literature will help one understand the complexities of managing a media program in which the professional media specialist is expected to "wear many hats." You may or may not agree with individual responses—as always, there is no single "right" solution.

The key terms related to most of the problems are "communication," "documentation," "justification," "publication and promotion," "long range planning," and "professional role." A common understanding of these terms must be shared by the administration, the media specialist, and the community. Agreeing on the meaning of those terms is a very difficult task for a profession that is one of the youngest in public education and that has evolved and changed dramatically over the past two decades.

The editors welcome reaction to any cases, as well as ideas for new cases. An open line of communication is available for any input to the editors. Contact Daniel Callison, at the School of Library and Information Science, Indiana University, Bloomington, IN 47405. Contact Jacqueline Morris at the Division of Federal Resources and School Improvement, 229 State House, Indianapolis, IN 46204.

Introduction

NEW NATIONAL GUIDELINES: INFORMATION POWER

The 1988 national guidelines for school library media programs, titled *Information Power: Guidelines for School Library Media Programs* (American Association of School Librarians and Association for Educational Communications and Technology) provide an excellent framework for background and ideas related to many of the cases presented here. We have attempted to identify problem areas and situations that develop in school library media programs during these early years of the "information age." Although the issues will still settle around personalities, funding, time, and the setting of priorities, the case studies place the discussion for these problems in the modern environment of the electronic media program. Two important considerations should always be kept in mind: (1) the *concept* of a modern school library media program and (2) the school library media specialist as an *interactive manager* of material and human resources.

THE CONCEPT

First, the modern school library media program is more than a building-level collection managed by a professional librarian. As Constance Champlin, coordinator of media services at Washington Township Schools in Indianapolis, constantly reminds us, the modern school library media program is a *concept*. It is a concept because the true, fully developed program does not exist. What we have are examples of exemplary services in some schools that have been developed by a few innovative and risk-taking media professionals. The school media program is a concept because it is still an innovation. Thinking of the media program as a concept rather than just a place or a location is necessary for the implementation of many of the management principles suggested in the case problems presented in this collection.

As a concept, the media program becomes integrated with the essential workings of curriculum design, teacher in-service, community involvement, and resource sharing. Thus, the media program is not just a collection of books, filmstrips, magazines, and other re-sources. The media program is the process of teachers and media professionals planning together, teaching together, and evaluating student performance together. The media program is the management of time and resources for the purpose of helping students gain access to the necessary materials.

As a concept, the media program means that the student should be challenged to make important choices in selection of facts and opinions wherever and whenever such decisions are necessary. Such a challenge should not be restricted to just the school library when the student is searching for resources for his or her report or term paper. Through many activities in the classroom and the community, the student can be placed in the position of needing to deal with information choices. The school library media program has evolved to its highest form when those who manage the program establish involvement in the classroom and community activities. Challenging students, teaching with fellow teachers, planning with administrators, and cooperating with other resource centers are the essential goals for the media program.

Management of a concept demands vision, the ability to verbalize what that vision is, and the ability to establish in a concrete manner a demonstration of what media services can do to improve the educational environment. This is a challenge that is very different from that of simply managing a circulation system or a collection of books. And even with case studies that involve seemingly routine management tasks, solutions must be sought that demonstrate clearly to fellow professionals the future potential for the school library media center. After all, current teachers, administrators, parents, and even school librarians have not really experienced the operation of the media center in its fullest dimensions. School libraries and the concepts of what a school library media program can be have changed since any of us last attended public schools.

THE INTERACTIVE MANAGER

Second, as presented in the new national guidelines, the school library media program is part of many networks, not just an information network as librarians commonly believe. Of course, the idea that school libraries should borrow and share resources is not new, but the move to share among libraries beyond the central school district is going to be difficult for many to implement. It is one thing to establish a service that allows teachers and students to borrow from others, and quite another thing to convince the administration that a role in such a network is to share what is owned locally with others.

The key term for this second line of thought is not networking but "interactiveness." Authors such as David Loertscher, Ken and

Carol-Ann Haycock, Phil Baker, Daniel Callison, Kay Vandergrift, Janet Stroud, and Philip Turner have used different terms to express the highest level of involvement of the school media specialist in the development of curriculum. In most areas the message is clear that school librarians are no longer just reacting to the curriculum demands, but are actively creating, with teachers, new instructional units and thus creating the need for more expanded information services. It is clear, however, in the 1988 guidelines, that another stage is evolving. School library media specialists have not only the responsibility to teach with teachers, but also the challenge to teach teachers how to gather, present, and evaluate information. The growing role is to educate teachers in the potential uses of information that lead to educational excellence.

James Liesener, for many years, and more recently Carol Collier Kuhlthau, have emphasized the importance of the role of the librarian as one who specializes in educating the patron or one who provides "information mediation." The media specialist is the model who leads in teaching and demonstrating the research process for both the student and teacher audience. An interactive approach demands that the school media specialist seek the leadership role and demonstrate information mediation expertise beyond the walls of the school library. There is a role to play in department meetings, board meetings, parent-teacher organizations, and joint meetings of the public-academic-school librarians. (If such meetings are not taking place, there is a role to play in creating an agenda for such cooperation and organizing meetings so communication can begin.)

Management at this level demands planning on a long-range basis, setting clear priorities with measurable goals and objectives, and delegating other tasks to staff. Most dramatically, management at this level may lead to a new meaning of staff itself, beyond the call for more volunteers, more clerical support, more student assistants. It may mean the *concentrated effort to teach teachers to be media specialists themselves and to assume more of the role of information manager in the classroom.* More than networking materials, the innovative manager of the school media program seeks to manage all resources, including human potential and skill, so that labor in all forms can be concentrated on the efforts to educate our youth as completely as possible in the information age. That's power with a capital P.

Contributors

The following individuals responded to the case studies presented in this book. These individuals represent a wide spectrum of professional experiences. The list includes practicing library/media specialists, district level directors, library educators, state department consultants, and graduate students.

ABS   Alice Bowie Steiner, Librarian, New Haven Middle School, New Haven, IN.

AH   Aileen Hemlick, Associate Professor and Department Chair, Department of Library Science and Information Service, Central Missouri State University, Warrensburg, MO.

AR   Alice Reck, Coordinator of Instructional Materials, Vigo County School Corporation, Terre Haute, IN.

AW   Arlene Wells, Media Specialist, Three Rivers Community Schools, Three Rivers, MI.

BJB   Betty Jo Buckingham, Consultant for Media Education, Iowa Department of Education, Des Moines, IA.

BNB   Beth Newberry Beckus, Librarian, Martin Luther King Jr. Middle School, Monterey Peninsula Unified School District, Monterey, CA.

CKD   Cynthia K. Dobrez, Youth Services Librarian, Oak Lawn Public Library, Oak Lawn, IL.

CLP   Clara Lee Parsons, Media Specialist, Lost Creek Elementary School, Vigo County School Corporation, Terre Haute, IN.

DC   Daniel Callison, Assistant Professor and Associate Dean, School of Library and Information Science, Indiana University, Bloomington, IN.

DP   Dorothy Pittman, Media Specialist, Greenville High School, Greenville, SC.

DPD   Donna Parkes DeGott, graduate student, School of Library and Information Science, Indiana University, Bloomington, IN.

DZP   Delores Zachary Pretlow, Supervisor of Media Services, Richmond Public Schools, Richmond, VA.

GH   Gloria Haycock, Media Coordinator, Northwestern Consolidated Schools, Fairland, IN.

HRA   Helen R. Adams, Librarian and Audiovisual Director, Rosholt High School, Rosholt, WI.

JAB   James A. Brown, Jr., Library Media Consultant, Ohio Department of Education, Columbus, OH.

JJ   Jane Johnson, Audiovisual Director, Carmel High School, Carmel, IN.

JK   Janice Krohne, Teacher, Abraham Lincoln Elementary School, Indianapolis, IN.

JM   Jacqueline Morris, Manager of the Learning Resources Unit, Indiana Department of Education, Indianapolis, IN.

JP   Janice Pickens, Media Specialist, Orleans High School, Orleans, IN.

JR   Julia Robinson, Media Specialist, Lawrence North High School, Indianapolis, IN.

JT   JoDell Thomas, Graduate Student, School of Library and Information Science, Indiana University, Bloomington, IN.

JWS   John W. Shearin, Media Consultant, Indiana Department of Education, Indianapolis, IN.

KC   Kathleen Cannallo, School Library Media Specialist, Soldotna, AK.

KM   Kenton Monjon, Teacher, Elkhart Central High School, Elkhart, IN.

KSB   Karen Sue Byes, English Department Chair, Maconaquah Middle School, Bunker Hill, IN.

LH   Lavon Hart, Director of District Audiovisual Services, Fort Wayne Community Schools, Fort Wayne, IN.

LYF   Lynette Yuki Furukawa, Graduate Student, University of Hawaii, Honolulu, HI.

MLS   Mary Lou Sproat, Media Specialist, Harrison Junior High, Merrillville, IN.

MMJ   Mary M. Jackson, Librarian, Argos Community Schools, Argos, IN.

MO   Mary Oppman, District Media Supervisor, Portage Township Schools, Portage, IN.

MP   Margaret Padilla, Librarian, Kauai Regional Library, Lawai, HI.

MPD   Margaret P. Dillner, Library Media Specialist, George Reed Middle School, New Castle, DE.

REW   Roger E. Whaley, Director of District Media Services, New Albany and Floyd County Schools, New Albany, IN.

SH   Shirley Harris, Media Specialist, Northwood Middle School, Fort Wayne, IN.

SJE   Susan Jane Eisman, Media Specialist, Terre Haute North Vigo High School, Terre Haute, IN.

SLR   Shirley L. Ross, Media Specialist, John Glenn School Corporation, Walkerton, IN.

VH   Vickie Hoff, Media Specialist, Rawlins High School, Rawlins, WY.

VLW   Virginia Lee Wallace, Media Specialist, Mauldin High School, Mauldin, SC.

Research Assistant: Sharon Roualet, Indiana University

Word Processing and Technical Assistant: Jennifer Hansen, Indiana University-Purdue University at Indianapolis.

Part I
Managing People for a Better Learning Environment

Case 1: Media Specialist Evaluation

Description —————————————————————————————

Every spring a review of each teacher in the elementary school is conducted by the principal. A standard form adopted from a national educators' group is provided. The principal visits each classroom for one hour, completes the form, and then schedules a conference with each teacher.

Professional skills which are listed on the form are:

a. Knowledge of subject matter
b. Planning and organization
c. Classroom management and control
d. Successful teaching techniques
e. Proper use of teaching aids and resources
f. The ability to motivate students
g. Resourcefulness and attention to details

This year the principal stops by the school media center and states to the media specialist, "I will plan to visit the media center next Monday at about 9 o'clock. But I don't plan to stay very long. Last year I didn't see anything I could really evaluate. There doesn't seem to be any teaching going on."

The media specialist was not comfortable with last year's review. She is completing a second year as the full-time professional for this elementary school media program, and she feels there are additional management tasks that she performs that should be evaluated as well as her teaching role. The principal never seems to have the time to observe such tasks and never seems to be available when the media specialist is actually teaching library skills. While not yet suggesting it to the principal, she thinks he might consider counting a planning session between herself and a classroom teacher as a skill that could be observed and evaluated.

What can the media specialist do to:

a. Bring to the principal's attention all of the jobs she performs in addition to teaching?
b. Demonstrate to the principal that she is as much a part of the teaching staff as any other member of the faculty?
c. Show there is more to the evaluation process than a once-a-year visit and a limited list of performance criteria?

Response

DEFINE WITH A JOB DESCRIPTION

The library media specialist should develop a list of responsibilities of her major roles: her role as teacher, her role as instructional consultant, her role as provider of access to resources, and her role as administrator.

During discussion with the administrator, the library media specialist should have several definite times in mind and a schedule in hand when she might be observed teaching. She might suggest that the principal stop in frequently for short periods to observe her involvement in the other areas.

During my years as an elementary school librarian, when my administrator used a form which only dealt with my teaching, I always signed the evaluation with an appendix: "This evaluation reflects only my teaching responsibility and does not evaluate consultive, administrative, or resource responsibilities."

The resource role is difficult for administrators to understand. I carried a tablet with me for one week and noted times and roles every half hour. I highlighted with different colors those times I was resourcing my patrons, consulting with teachers, administering my library, and teaching students. It was a very useful item when my administrator pointed to my teaching schedule and said I had plenty of time for clerical tasks with no clerical help. *(MP)*

TAKE EVERY OPPORTUNITY TO SHOW YOUR WORTH

The problem is that most school districts use a common evaluation form for all personnel who work under a "teacher's contract." The limited structure and scope of the forms and the fact that so few principals have a thorough understanding of the total responsibilities involved in managing a media center are frustrating to the library media specialist. Her task is to change her principal's overall view of the media center.

The media specialist should approach the principal several days before his planned visit and tell him when her next formal instructional lesson will be, thus offering him a chance to view her in a situation common to his normal evaluation pattern.

After the visit, but before the conference, she should prepare a detailed list of all media activities she is currently doing.

She should contact all local, state, and national professional organizations and media professionals in other school corporations for their input and evaluation, especially those discussed in publications by the National Association of Elementary School Principals. During this part of the discussion, she should begin to involve the principal in one aspect of her duties. Selection of materials is a good place to start.

She should now tell the principal about, or show him, the forms used for evaluation that she has collected (see figures 1 and 2 for sample evaluations forms).

Ideally, evaluations should be an opportunity for the principal and all teachers to share problems and suggest alternatives leading to improvement. The atmosphere should be conducive to open discussion. In the case of those of us who are media specialists, the principal must be tactfully educated to changes in our profession. Remember, most unjustified or unfair evaluations of media specialists do not occur intentionally, but happen because the media specialist fails to keep the principal up to date on developments and plans relating to the media program and their effect on the total educational program within the building. *(SJE)*

Figure 1. Library Media Specialist Evaluation

In the space before each statement, place the number which best describes performance:

Outstanding	Satisfactory	Needs Improvement
5–4	3–2	1

I. The library media center is easily accessible, flexible, and physically attractive.

_____ The library media specialist (LMS) makes every effort to meet student needs.

_____ The LMS exhibits a pleasant, friendly, accepting attitude toward teachers and students.

_____ The LMS demonstrates enthusiasm in his or her work.

_____ The LMS continually implements and reevaluates the procedures and policies of the media program.

_____ The LMS adds many decorative touches to make the library an inviting place.

_____ The LMS keeps the library open before and after school as well as during the day.

_____ The LMS promotes an informal atmosphere in the library.

_____ The LMS is willing to change any regulation which is found to be against the best interests of teachers and students.

_____ The LMS is receptive to innovative teaching methods which involve changes in the way the library is used.

_____ The LMS encourages the circulation of all library materials to classrooms and homes.

_____ The LMS cooperates with the changing utilization of staff and offers to serve as a member of teaching teams.

_____ The LMS encourages the use of the library by individuals and small groups coming from study hall and/or classrooms.

_____ The LMS supervises students using the media center and encourages them to make constructive use of their time.

_____ The LMS works with teachers and principals to develop a flexible scheduling of classes to the library.

_____ The LMS capably administers the budget.

_____ The LMS trains and supervises clerks and student assistants in paraprofessional and clerical tasks.

_____ The LMS continues to acquire knowledge through inservice and/or academic courses.

_____ The LMS assumes an active role in professional organizations and activities.

II. The library media center serves as a centralized multimedia resource center.

_____ The LMS is thoroughly familiar with the school curriculum, with teaching methods, and with student, faculty, and community interest so that he or she can develop an excellent, functional collection of materials.

_____ The LMS organizes all materials for quick and easy access. He catalogs and inventories materials which are on permanent loan to departments and classrooms.

_____ The LMS spends much time becoming familiar with the content of all media in the library.

_____ The LMS provides materials for the atypical student—the slow learner, the gifted, the nonverbal, culturally disadvantaged, etc.

_____ The LMS knows and keeps on hand the approved selection aids for all media and orders new materials only after consulting these lists and/or after personal examination.

_____ The LMS weeds the collection frequently to discard out-of-date and worn-out materials.

_____ The LMS urges that all supplementary instructional materials be selected, ordered, and inventoried through the library.

III. The library media center serves as a learning center which implements the goals of the total school program.

_____ The LMS maintains good working relations with staff members.

_____ The LMS considers technical and routine duties subordinate to working with teachers and students.

_____ The LMS is willing to serve on district committees such as curriculum, film, block grant, equipment, etc.

_____ The LMS assists teachers and students in the construction of teaching materials.

_____ The LMS keeps informed concerning classroom activities.

_____ The LMS, individually and in department meetings, plans with the teachers.

_____ The LMS encourages students to become independent in their use of the library materials.

_____ The LMS teaches library skills cooperatively with teachers as the need arises.

_____ The LMS extends his or her services into the classroom, teaching library skills, giving book talks, and finding ways to integrate the use of print and nonprint materials.

_____ The LMS keeps students and teachers informed of new materials received and innovations in library services and educational practices.

_____ The LMS provides materials and helps plan programs to promote the professional growth of the school staff.

_____ The LMS works individually with students, helping them define a field of inquiry, locate information, and evaluate pertinent data.

IV. The library media center serves to promote the student's personal development.

_____ The LMS publicizes library services and materials in many inventive, attractive ways which are related to student's interests and mores.

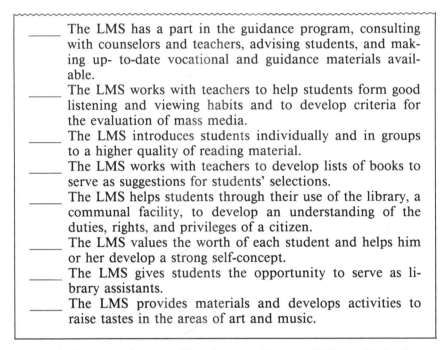

_____ The LMS has a part in the guidance program, consulting with counselors and teachers, advising students, and making up- to-date vocational and guidance materials available.

_____ The LMS works with teachers to help students form good listening and viewing habits and to develop criteria for the evaluation of mass media.

_____ The LMS introduces students individually and in groups to a higher quality of reading material.

_____ The LMS works with teachers to develop lists of books to serve as suggestions for students' selections.

_____ The LMS helps students through their use of the library, a communal facility, to develop an understanding of the duties, rights, and privileges of a citizen.

_____ The LMS values the worth of each student and helps him or her develop a strong self-concept.

_____ The LMS gives students the opportunity to serve as library assistants.

_____ The LMS provides materials and develops activities to raise tastes in the areas of art and music.

Reprinted with permission from Mary Oppman, Director of Library Media, Portage Township Schools, Portage, IN.

PUBLIC RELATIONS

This program could probably be helped by some aggressive public relations on the part of the media specialist. Depending on the flexibility of her program, all sorts of solutions come to mind. In my experience, I have worked with fourth- through sixth-grade classes on dramatizations of familiar stories which we then invited the lower elementary grades and special education classes to attend. A copy of the formal invitation sent to teachers of these classes was also sent not only to the principal, but to key people at the central office such as the library director, elementary curriculum supervisor, and superintendent. When the students wrote and illustrated their own books, copies of the best were sent to the principal, who also served as a judge. In a book report marathon, he was asked to listen to younger students tell him about the books they had read. Whenever anything at all unusual was going on in the media center, even if it was just a particularly good film we had borrowed, the principal received a personal invitation. When I felt the fourth-grade students were well drilled in library skills, I invited him to sit in on an oral test. At year-end he received a written report of not only circulation statistics

Figure 2. Delaware Performance Appraisal System—Specialist Appraisal Summary

For <u>non-tenured specialists</u>, the Specialist Appraisal Summary is completed every year. It is based on a minimum of three (3) interim appraisals. At least two (2) of the three (3) interim appraisals must include announced observations. For <u>tenured specialists</u>, the Specialist Appraisal Summary is completed every other year. It is based on a minimum of two (2) interim appraisals per year which will include one (1) announced observation.

<u>Directions</u>: 1. Complete the identification information on the top of the next page.

2. Transfer each of the six (6) category assessments and the overall interim appraisal from each interim appraisal. Code "very good" as "VG," "Good" as "G" and "unsatisfactory" as "U." Be sure to enter each assessment in the appropriate column. Also mark whether the observation was announced (A) or unannounced (U).

3. Determine the evaluation assessment for each of the six (6) categories of specialist behaviors as "very good" (VG), "good" (G), or "unsatisfactory" (U). The assessment should be based on the individual interim appraisals for each category, narrative comments, and other relevant documentation. The evaluation assessment is not an average of the interim appraisals. Be sure to consider performance changes over time.

4. Determine the overall appraisal based on the pattern of assessments by indicating whether the specialist is "very good" (VG), "good" (G), or "unsatisfactory" (U). The overall appraisal is not an average of individual evaluation assessments or overall interim appraisals. It includes individual evaluation assessments, overall interim appraisals, narrative comments, and other relevant documentation. Be sure to consider performance changes over time.

5. Provide commendations and/or recommendations for the overall appraisal in narrative form. For each category assessed "very good" or "unsatisfactory," explain the assessment and provide commendations or specific recommendations for specialist improvement.

Reprinted with permission from The Delaware Department of Public Instruction.

Figure 2. Delaware Performance Appraisal System—Specialist Appraisal Summary (cont.)

Specialist Area:_____

Name:_____   Tenure Status:_____

Evaluator:_____   School Year(s):_____

School:_____   District:_____

Categories of Specialist Behavior	Interim Appraisals								Evaluation Assessments
	1_*	2_	3_	4_	5_	6_	7_	8_	
I. Planning/Preparation									
II. Work Area Management									
III. Specialist/Student/Staff Interaction									
IV. Techniques and Activities									
V. Performance Monitoring/ Feedback/Evaluation									
VI. Related Responsibilities									
OVERALL APPRAISAL									

*Announced/Unannounced

Reprinted with permission from The Delaware Department of Public Instruction.

Figure 2. Delaware Performance Appraisal System—Specialist Appraisal Summary (cont.)

(For Announced Visits)

Date Submitted to
Teacher/Specialist_____
Date of Visit_____

Name:_____School:_____

Evaluator:_____Assignment:_____

Please complete the following information and return to the Evaluator at least 48 hours before the scheduled date of the visit.

Pre-conference Requested?   Yes ____   No ____   By Whom?_____

1. What are the objectives of the lesson, activities and/or unit?

2. What teaching/learning activities, and methods or specialist activity will be used?

3. How will student progress be monitored?

** Are there any group or individual characteristics or circumstances of which the evaluator should be aware?   (Unusual behaviors, grouping interactions, students leaving class during the period, lab work, etc.)

Date Returned to Evaluator:_____   **Date of Pre-conference:_____

Teacher/Specialist Signature:_____

Evaluator's Signature:_____

Copies To: Teacher/Specialist
            Evaluator
**Optional

Reprinted with permission from The Delaware Department of Public Instruction.

and books added or lost but also highlights of the year and plans for improving services next year. *(JR)*

DOCUMENT WITH PEER TESTIMONY AND INVOLVEMENT

If a teacher stopped in to comment on how helpful the media center was, I asked her or him to stop by the principal's office and tell him too. After the yearly state conference, the principal received a written report on the highlights of helpful workshops I had attended. I also asked him for a copy of the curriculum guides in each subject area, so I could contact the teachers about units they were teaching and offer them resources. At ordering time, I asked teachers to prioritize choices I had made, and offer their suggestions for other materials. When I sent the order request to him, I noted which materials had been recommended by teachers. I also spent a lot of time recruiting parent volunteers to help in the library, and since they had to check in through the office, he had a running count of the parent involvement, which was a direct result of my effort. When the school district photographer came around to take pictures (teachers were asked to submit photograph suggestions routinely prior to his visits), I always had a media center shot in the requests. *(JR)*

DOCUMENT WITH STATISTICAL EVIDENCE

While keeping records might seem time-consuming, it can pay dividends at evaluation time.

Using forms that show when classes are scheduled for the media center, forms that show when television taping or broadcasting is planned, and forms that schedule computer use are several ways in which program planning, program evaluation, and time management can be accomplished. These records also show how often the media center is being used, by whom, and for what purposes (see Figure 3 for a sample teacher planning form).

These forms and records, along with your providing the principal with notes from conferences of interest and your doing mini-workshops with teachers, will ensure your recognition as a vital part of the teaching staff. *(SH)*

REFLECT TEACHING AND ADMINISTRATION ROLES IN THE EVALUATION FORM

A media director in a large school district observed that one of the library media specialists in the high school was being treated in the manner described in the case. At the next district meeting of the library media specialists, she requested that as a group we address the issue of evaluation of library media specialists. Members of the group agreed to work on the development of an evaluation instrument. They read several articles on the subject. They took two instruments and developed one that applied to their situation. One copy of the instrument was sent to the teachers' bargaining unit and another to the assistant superintendent, with the request that it, rather than the standard teacher evaluation form, be used. To date, the only comment returned has been that it is very detailed. The library media specialists expect it to be accepted and implemented this year. *(MO)*

Figure 3. Northwood Media Center, Teacher Planning Sheet for Media Center and Related Work

Teacher's Name: _____ Subject Area: _____

Dates of Assignment: FROM _____ TO: _____

Number of classes involved in your assignment: _____

Explanation of overall assignment:

1. What materials do you expect students to use in the Media Center?

   Encyclopedias ___   Vertical File ___   Computer Software __

   Magazines ___   Maps ___   SIRS ___
   Books ___   Audiovisuals ___   Other ___

2. Would you like the Media teacher to help you in any way?

   YES ___   NO ___   UNDECIDED __

3. Please find attached: _____ a list of _____

   _____ a copy of the student's worksheet

   _____ other (please explain if necessary)

Today's Date: _____

Reprinted with permission from Shirley A. Harris, Northwood Middle School, Fort Wayne, IN.

EDUCATE THE PRINCIPAL BY COMMUNICATION

The media specialist should find an opportunity to discuss her evaluation with the principal and then extend an invitation to him to visit at a specific time to observe her teaching a class, and again at a time to see her teaching one student. (For the whole-class session, I would suggest she teach a search strategy or a fascinating reference book, either of which has a direct bearing on what students are doing in "academics." For the one-student session, I recommend she teach how to use a particular piece of equipment.)

Further, the library media specialist should point out the number of learning centers established and the environment created to stimulate independent study, browsing, and inquiry. The library media specialist may also suggest to the principal that he may be particularly interested in the evaluation form in the April 1984 issue of the *NASSP Bulletin* and the article "Evaluating the School Librarian" since it was developed by his peers. *(MO)*

COMMUNICATE YOUR MISSION

This media specialist has a communication problem. If she was not comfortable with last year's review, why has she allowed an entire year to go by without doing something to improve her situation? It is stated that the principal "never seems to have the time to observe such tasks and never seems to be available when the media specialist is actually teaching library skills." Has she communicated clearly to him that she would like him to observe her teaching? Has she talked with him about the management tasks which she performs and would like to have evaluated?

1. Establish guidelines for evaluation, by:
   a. Using a job description
   b. Locating evaluation criteria and forms from others
   c. Reading professional articles
2. Define the functions of the media specialist, by:
   a. Writing a mission statement with goals, objectives, and activities
   b. Having the mission statement approved by the principal as his criteria for evaluation
3. Emphasize the media specialist as teacher, by:
   a. Defining the term "teaching"
   b. Showing the media specialist's role as a member of the teaching team *(MP)*

TEACHERS AND MORE

Media specialists are teachers and much more. This media specialist needs a job description as a first step. The next step is to meet with the principal to set up a performance evaluation for the coming year with specific goals and the activities to be observed as bases of evaluation. The new national guidelines, *Information Power: Guidelines for School Library Media Programs,* published in 1988, describes the various roles, including the instructional design role, the teaching role, and the information management role. All of these are necessary for a successful library media program. The competencies outlined should be brought to the principal's attention as the criteria advocated by the national association.

The suggested peer evaluation is an excellent way to demonstrate the media specialist's value to the teaching staff. Keeping a record of the units worked on with teachers and statistics that measure output will help convince administrators of your worth. A well-planned performance evaluation will also show this principal that a once-a-year visit with a set of criteria that doesn't fit the role simply isn't enough for any teacher evaluation. *(JM)*

BIBLIOGRAPHY

American Association of School Librarians and Association for Educational Communications and Technology. *Information Power: Guidelines for School Library Media Programs.* Chicago: American Library Association, 1988.
See pages 64–65. "Since most principals do not have experience in the library media field as they do in classroom teaching, it is particularly important that the role and function of the library media specialist be clearly defined and jointly agreed upon."
The Book Report 6(2) (1987).
This is a theme issue on evaluation and professional development for the school media specialist. Articles of interest include "Goal Setting and Evaluation," "Performance-Based Evaluation," and "Evaluating Librarians: Aren't We Different from Teachers?"
Chisholm, Margaret E., and Donald P. Ely. *Media Personnel in Education; A Competency Approach.* Englewood Cliffs, NJ: Prentice-Hall, 1976.
Deals with the role of the media professional, user needs, and explanations of functions and competencies. Chapters devoted to each of 10 functions include a description of the function and related competencies, a list of resources for gaining the competencies, a mastery item, and the response to the mastery item.

DiPaolo, Andy. "A Self-Assessment Approach to Performance Appraisal." *Media Management Journal* 5(3) (1986): 6–8.
This article describes a performance review instrument using a self-assessment approach to evaluate the skills and behaviors applicable to management and supervisory roles of the school library media specialist.

Haycock, Ken. "7 Steps to Developing Support from School Principals." *Emergency Librarian* 15(1) (1987): 25.
Ken Haycock's suggestions are always valuable. On one page he lists the best approaches to gain favor with the school administration: Plan a strategy, confer regularly, be specific, be professional, involve the administrator, be visible, and communicate effectively.

Loertscher, David V., Blanche Woolls, Russell Blumeyer, Paul Spurlock, and Betty Jo Buckingham. *Media Center Program Evaluation Document for Iowa Area Education Agencies*. Des Moines, IA: Iowa Department of Public Instruction, 1979.
A fine group of experienced media educators and media supervisors put together this notebook for evaluation of the media specialist and media program which serves a region of a state. The questions raised in 1979 are still of value today. Often the evaluation is based on an "evolution" of the media program as it grows and matures to provide more services. Often the professional status of the media specialist evolves in the same manner.

Pfister, Fred C., Joyce P. Vincelette, and Jonnie B. Sprimont. "An Integrated Performance Evaluation and Program Evaluation System." *School Library Media Quarterly* 14(2) (1986): 61–68.
This is the most recent of a series of articles from media educators at Florida State. Professor Pfister has field tested a number of instruments which are useful for improving the image and performance of the school media specialist. Each of the following references leads to background information on the project:

Pfister, Fred C., and Joyce P. Vincelette. "Model Job Description and Evaluation Standards for School Media Specialists." 1983. ERIC document ED 228 325.
Appraisal instruments are included for several different size media programs and for elementary and secondary media programs.

Pfister, Fred C., and Nelson Towle. "A Practical Model for a Developmental Appraisal Program for School Library Media Specialists." *School Library Media Quarterly* 11(2) (1983): 111–21.

Vincelette, Joyce P., and Fred C. Pfister. "Improving Performance Appraisal in Libraries." *Library and Information Science Research* 6(2) (1984): 191–203.

Pichette, William H. "A Checklist for Principals: Evaluating the School Librarian." *NASSP Bulletin* (April 1984): 124–30.
A list of tasks is given along with the suggestion that both the principal and the librarian complete the Professional Growth Planning Form. This list can serve as an agenda for setting professional goals.

Staples, Susan E. "60 Competency Ratings for School Media Specialists." *Instructional Innovator* 26(9) (1981): 19–23.
A report of a statewide survey in Texas which asked learning resources specialists to (1) rate the importance of 60 competency statements describing functional job-related skills, (2) rate their own ability to perform these functions, and (3) indicate where they felt continuing education was needed.

Yesner, Bernice L., and Hilda L. Jay. *The School Administrator's Guide to Evaluating Library Media Programs.* Hamden, CT: Library Professional Publications, 1987.
Provides forms for evaluation of the facility as well as evaluation of the professional media center staff. Although the guide is aimed at the principal, the media specialist should be ready to show where many areas suggested in this plan should be adjusted in order to give a more complete picture of the many professional responsibilities of the school media specialist.

For additional ideas for evaluation forms in areas for both personnel and program evaluation contact:

National Study of School Evaluation
5201 Leesburg Pike
Falls Church, VA 22041

Case 2: What Do They Do, Anyway?

Description

The pressures from rising expenses to run a school corporation and the reluctance to increase taxes have brought the Pixel County School Board to the bottom line: Cut staff, courses, or services. Enrollment declined in the Pixel County School District from 1972 to 1982, but it has leveled off for the past few years. Reducing the teaching staff is one option that remains low since most of the reductions during the years the enrollment declined were made by "riffing" teachers. New mandates from the state legislature following discussion of issues raised by such publications as *A Nation at Risk* have established several reforms in the public schools. The most notable has been Operation Prime Time, which established a required ratio in grades K–4 of no more than 20 students to 1 teacher.

Private discussions among board members have touched on various areas for decreasing funding. These include special service teaching positions such as art, music, and media specialists. Some discussion has also been directed toward extending this year's cycle of new textbook adoption for two more years and also reducing funds provided for supplemental instructional materials. An area that has received a great deal of attention as a potential way to reduce expenses is school media services. One high school media specialist is scheduled to retire this coming spring. Failing to fill that position would leave two full-time media positions in a high school of 2,400 students. There were no media specialists removed from the high school during the period the regular teaching staff was reduced.

However, the most vulnerable area for media specialists seems to be the elementary schools. Of the eight elementary schools, seven have full-time media specialists. The other is a small rural elementary school which has a library/media center that is managed by a paid clerk and "supervised" by the principal. Three of the current elementary media specialists are within one year of retirement.

At the March board meeting, one board member recommends, "Let's not replace those elementary school librarians with high-priced people coming out of the university. Let's put adult clerks in there for one-fourth the cost, keep a couple of the current librarians to oversee the ordering of books and such, and send the others to the junior high school and the senior high school. Now that's a savings of nearly $50,000 a year. I see no problem. Besides, what could a librarian do in an elementary school all day every day anyhow? I don't even remember having any around this district 15 years ago when my kids were going through school."

A second board member proposes, "We can save some money in the area of periodicals in the high school and junior high. It's only about $3,500, but if we simply cut the money invested in newspapers and magazines and allow parents to donate their old magazines to the school, we can save a little. Besides, I can't see that any of our kids will be denied much when the newspaper they get at school is a couple of days old."

A third board member indicates agreement with both proposals, and concludes, "I don't know what school librarians do anyhow."

As one of the school media specialists in this district, how would you:

a. Respond to the board?
b. Involve the others in your response to the board?
c. Seek to guard against such a line of argument from board members ever taking place again?

Response

ASK TO MEET WITH THE BOARD

I would ask for either a public or private meeting with the board members and/or their designated representatives to discuss and demonstrate the many services that elementary school media specialists provide. At this meeting I would tell about the many different activities that take place in the media center that I serve. I would bring a slide presentation to emphasize the library/media center as the busiest and most important place in school. *(CLP)*

RELATE THE PHILOSOPHY OF THE MODERN SCHOOL LIBRARY MEDIA CENTER

When I was first hired, my job was that of school librarian. Library collections consisted mainly of books, and students were allowed to visit the library with their class once every 2 weeks for a 30-minute time period.

The library program has evolved over the years, and we now have an "open door" flexible program, which means that students are allowed to use the library/media center whenever they have their teacher's permission. The flexible program allows the students to individually visit the library/media center two or three times a week and some students check out books and media every day. Some students who are working on research-type projects may use the center for 2 or 3 hours every day with the guidance of a professional media specialist. Several times during the day, the media specialist is involved with storytime for the early primary classes and with teaching library and reference skills to upper primary and intermediate classes. During these times, individual students from several other classrooms will also be using the media center for a variety of purposes and to look for materials on their own.

I would point out that my job description has changed tremendously due to the advent of the computer and technology age. Among other tasks, my job involves instruction in the use of computers, videotaping equipment, laminating equipment, film projectors, opaque projectors, overhead projectors, 35mm cameras, film processing, duplicating, and editing equipment, audiodubbing equipment, etc. This instruction in the use of the equipment involves not only the faculty, but students as well. *(CLP)*

INVOLVE CONSTITUENTS TO SHOW SUPPORT

I would invite teachers, parents, and students to accompany me to this meeting with the board. Some ways we might show support for the program include these:

1. Each library media specialist should present his or her reading programs that show significant achievement in student test scores. These programs might be presented in the form of posters, slides, or student work,
2. Teachers could present data showing how the media center is an integral part of their curriculum,
3. PTO volunteers might present past evidence of the impact that the qualified media specialist and the elementary media program had on present junior high/senior high students. *(MLS)*

OVERWHELM THEM WITH STATISTICS

Point out student use, circulation, and special programs. Although we have entered the technology age, we still like to think that the media center is "user friendly," for our circulation statistics are overwhelming. Circulation statistics show that our elementary school students use 10 times as many materials per week as high school students.

Through my efforts, students have participated successfully in March of Dimes Readathon and Campbell's Labels for Education, produced the school yearbook, participated in the statewide Young Hoosier Book Award program, promoted the local STP reading program, and promoted Children's Book Week in November and National Library Week in April of each school year.

A quarter of the student body is involved in the media fair, entering over 40 different projects. I am involved in coaching them in eight different categories: (1) computer programming, (2) video production, (3) film production, (4) slide/filmstrip production, (5) audio production, (6) transparency production, (7) photography, and (8) multivisual media. *(MLS)*

POINT OUT THE DIFFERENCES IN A PROFESSIONAL POSITION AND A CLERICAL POSITION

Use job descriptions:

1. To present the media program as administered by a qualified media specialist and to show the media program as administered by a clerk.
2. To point out that a clerk cannot be expected to do a media specialist's job for clerk's pay and without the preparation for the position that a degreed professional requires.

Remind the board that the 40 successful media fair projects mentioned above required that the media specialist remain at school until about 5:30 p.m. every day for approximately the 2 months that preceded the media fair (something a clerical aide would not be inclined to do unless he or she were compensated for this extra time).

After presenting the above-mentioned information to the board members for their consideration, I might also suggest that it is in their sphere of action to consider employing both a full-time clerical person and a media professional to staff each elementary media center to better accomplish the above services.

To guard against this line of reasoning ever happening again:

1. Make the library media center indispensable and develop visible programs.

2. Develop reading appreciation programs that have specific goals but leave room for individuality.
3. Develop an elementary curriculum that includes the library research skills essential to writing skills, and tie these into proficiencies.
4. Develop a computer-assisted tutoring program that is administered in the media center. *(MLS)*

ENGAGE IN A STRONG PUBLIC RELATIONS CAMPAIGN

Promote! Promote! Promote effectively! In an effort to promote our worth, we need to:

1. Contribute noteworthy articles to our local PTA newsletters, newspapers, journals, etc.;
2. Encourage parent volunteers to help in our media centers, which will provide them with the opportunity to see for themselves the vast amount of student involvement and activities that take place there;
3. Serve on curriculum and other school corporation committees;
4. Become active in worthy community organizations as well as the PTA;
5. Promote Media Fair participation with students and teachers;
6. Continually inform staff, teachers, and students about new materials;
7. Never hesitate to invite board members to view media center activities;
8. Inform board members when students have made outstanding achievements through using media center activities, i.e., Media Fair projects;
9. Never turn down an opportunity to talk about the media center and its various activities when asked to make a presentation to a community organization. *(CLP)*

BIBLIOGRAPHY

American Association of School Librarians and Association for Educational Communications and Technology. *Information Power: Guidelines for School Library Media Programs.* Chicago: American Library Association, 1988.
See pages 26–55. "A fundamental responsibility of the library media specialist is to provide the leadership and expertise necessary to ensure that the library program is an integral part of the instructional program of the school." Appendix E, pages 149–54, provides a listing of selected research studies. These studies are grouped under the following headings: "Elementary Library Media Programs," "Secondary Library Media Pro-

grams," "Post-Secondary Education," "Education of Library Media Personnel," and "Curricular Role of the Library Media Specialist." Evidence from nearly 40 studies since the 1960s to the mid-1980s helps to support the following conclusions:

a. There is significant improvement in student reading scores, study skills, and teacher and student access to the library in schools with library media programs staffed by full-time professionals.
b. Students demonstrated a significant increase in the ability to solve problems and locate, organize, and evaluate information through instruction by professional full-time librarians.
c. Full-time librarians with graduate degrees offer more extensive services and their libraries are more heavily used than libraries operated by lesser-educated staff or limited clerical support only.

Baldridge, Sherie W., and Marsha D. Broadway. "Who Needs an Elementary School Librarian?" *Principal* 67(2) (1987): 37–40.
Provides some ideas for a defense against cutting funds which support school library services. Arguments are based on "relationships" between a strong school library media program and academic excellence.

Barron, Daniel D. "Communicating What SLM Specialists Do: The Evaluation Process." *School Library Journal* 33(7) (1987): 95–99.
Points emphasized include setting objectives and communicating the process of successfully meeting those objectives. Such objectives should be based on the educational needs of the school.

Callison, Daniel. "Evaluator and Educator: The School Media Specialist." *Tech Trends* 32(5) (1987): 95–97.
This is an outline of the professional role of the media specialist which includes not only teaching students, but also teaching fellow teachers. Such "higher level" instruction includes planning curriculum, evaluating learning activities on an equal basis with teachers, and demonstrating to teachers how information skills can be integrated into classroom assignments.

———. "Justification for Action in Future School Library Media Programs." *School Library Media Quarterly* 12(3) (1984): 205–11.
A plan which calls for identification of a few most important goals is suggested. Meeting these goals should generate tangible products which establish credibility for the overall program.

Didier, Elaine K. Macklin. "Relationships between Student Achievement in Reading and Library Media Programs and Personnel." Dissertation. University of Michigan, 1982.
Major hypotheses tested:

a. Student attainment of reading and study skills will be significantly greater in districts with a full-time media specialist in each building.
b. There is a significant positive relationship between education of media personnel and their curricular role.
c. There is a significant positive relationship between the presence of a full-time media specialist and student access to the media center.

Didier provides a summary of her research and other related studies in "Research on the Impact of School Library Media Programs on Student Achievement—Implications for School Library Media Professionals." In *School Library Media Annual 1984,* edited by Shirley L. Aaron and Pat R. Scales, pp. 343–61, Littleton, CO: Libraries Unlimited, 1984.

Drexel Library Quarterly 21(2) (1985).

This special issue,"Measures of Excellence for School Media Centers," edited by David V. Loertscher, is a major source of techniques which can lead to the librarian gathering tangible evidence of his or her role. Methods are given which lead to measurable products of the media program. The philosophy is accountability based on "outputs."

Ely, Donald P. *Public Relations for School Media Programs: An ERIC Fact Sheet.* 1981. ERIC document ED 232 704.

Designed for elementary and secondary school library media personnel. This document emphasizes that because library media programs are vulnerable to budget cuts, the need exists to educate those making fiscal decisions on the role of these materials in the curriculum. A five-step guide for communicating information is outlined: (1) Determine who sends the message; (2) decide the content of the message; (3) identify the audience; (4) seek vehicles for communication; and (5) determine the objective of the message and methods to evaluate its effectiveness.

Kulleseid, Eleanor R. *Beyond Survival to Power for School Library Media Professionals.* Hamden, CT: Library Professional Publications, 1985.

Although Kulleseid's examples seem to be limited to the New York City area, she gives a great deal of insight as to how the power structures evolve within public school districts. From her case studies, many elementary school library media specialists will gain ideas as to how to "survive and even thrive despite pressures and financial cutbacks."

Liesener, James W. "Learning at Risk: School Library Media Programs in an Information World." *School Library Media Quarterly* 14(1) (1985): 11–20.

Focuses on the role of school library media programs in the fostering of lifelong learning and the development of information skills.

Loertscher, David V., May Lein Ho, and Melvin M. Bowie. "Exemplary Elementary Schools and Their Library Media Centers: A Research Report." School Library Media Quarterly. 15(3) (1987): 147-53.

Quality media programs included inservice training for teachers in effective use of materials, special programming for students, development of independent study programs for credit, and activities involving students in the production and use of nonprint media. The report states, however, that if adequate staff and funding are not provided, such quality media programs are not likely. Full-time clerical assistance is necessary in order for the full-time library media specialist to take an effective professional role.

Turner, Philip M. *Helping Teachers Teach.* Littleton, CO: Libraries Unlimited, 1985.

As summarized in its title, this useful collection of exercises discusses the most important role of the media specialist. This book is also useful to those who wish to document such a team-teaching role.

————. "The Future of School Library Media Preparation Programs: Perils and Potentials." *Top of the News* 43(2) (1987): 161–65.

A model is proposed which defines three purposes of school library media programs and provides a template against which specific professional programs can be scrutinized and improved.

Wilson Library Bulletin 56(6) (1982): 415–33.

This issue features four articles which describe a "second revolution" in school library media programs. This change is the movement toward curriculum development leadership. David Loertscher, Retta Patrick, and Janet Stroud combine ideas to show the impact of this change. Specific instructional media program examples show the extent of involvement of the school library media specialist in the curriculum of the school.

Case 3: A Censoring Volunteer

Description

Mary Greenwall, media specialist at Washington Junior High School, has invested a great deal of time and effort in building a good parent volunteer program. She has a full crew of parents, including one father and two grandparents, who provide time to help on such tasks as mending books, printing a media center newsletter, and even tracking down materials from other libraries.

Over the years, Ms. Greenwall's volunteer system has evolved so that one volunteer serves as the coordinator. Her responsibilities include calling a substitute volunteer when one is ill for the day or for some other reason cannot come to school. The coordinator also is responsible for training the new volunteers and moving them into higher-level tasks as they become acquainted with the media center and as the media specialist becomes acquainted with the volunteer. The first job for new volunteers is to help read shelves and to shelve books.

Maureen Paulsen was a new volunteer. She has two children in the junior high and one at the senior high school. She had never volunteered in any capacity with the public schools before. Mrs. Paulsen came to the media center twice a week, 3 hours each Monday and Thursday mornings.

The third Thursday morning Mrs. Paulsen did not arrive at her usual 8:30 a.m. time. She had not notified the coordinator that she would be late or absent. At 8:45 a call came from Sandra Drennan, the school principal. Ms. Greenwall was requested to meet with the principal immediately.

The school media specialist walked into the office to find seven library books stacked neatly on the principal's desk. "Mrs. Paulsen came to see me yesterday afternoon," said the principal.

"What did she want?" asked Ms. Greenwall.

"She handed me these books from our library and had a list of about 40 other book titles she says a local parent group she supports

has decided to seek out and remove from libraries and bookstores."
The principal gave Ms. Greenwall a copy of the list titled "Bad Books
for Boys and Girls," and then continued to describe the incident with
Mrs. Paulsen. "She removed four of these books from our library
because they were on the list, and she removed the other three
because she says they were close to being the same kind of 'trash.'
She told me that she wants to continue to search the collection until
she has found all of the 'rotten apples in the basket.' We discussed
the situation for about 45 minutes, and I asked her to cite specific
passages she had read or to describe specific content to which she
objected. She had read none of these books. You know I don't mind
parents raising a question about what we do around here as long as
they are prepared and have done as much homework as the kids and
our teachers. The short of it is, I asked her to leave the books and I
would return them to you. I asked her not to continue as a volunteer
for us in any manner. Please take these back and have them
reshelved."

As the school media specialist, consider the following:

a. Discuss the role of volunteers in public schools. What should
   be the division between the professional staff and parent volunteer?
b. Should parents have a voice in questioning educational materials?
c. Should parents have a role in evaluating library materials in
   the same manner they help evaluate textbooks?
d. Should the media specialist have been involved more in the
   decision-making process, or do you feel the principal took the
   proper steps?
e. What role does a collection policy play in this situation?

Response

NOTHING SOLVED, MORE PROBLEMS CREATED

Local citizens should be encouraged to become involved in the
schools; however, the motivations for volunteering should be carefully
investigated. Intensive training and task assignments by professional
personnel are imperative. Ms. Greenwall has engaged in good management practices in permitting volunteers to assume increasingly
responsible roles; but she must clearly define the difference between
professional and volunteer responsibilities. One excellent guideline to
follow, if at all possible, is to assign volunteers to school buildings
where their own children or grandchildren are *not* in attendance.

Mrs. Paulsen, just as any other citizen, has the right to challenge the inclusion of materials in the library. Every school should have a board-adopted selection and collection development policy that ensures the right to challenge and defines the process for requesting reconsideration of materials. Perhaps Mrs. Paulsen took the books to the principal because she assumed that was the correct procedure. It would appear, however, that the problem goes far beyond Mrs. Paulsen and that there is a systematic plan to purge the library. Placement of a volunteer in the library was a very clever maneuver. At any rate, the principal's behavior left something to be desired, even though her defense of the right to read is laudable. Mrs. Drennan, the principal, instantly created an environment of hostility by "firing" Mrs. Paulsen. This may well cause a defensive reaction by other volunteers and community members and certainly positions the local parent group in a fighting posture.

Ms. Greenwall should have been consulted before any action was taken. She may have been able to engage Mrs. Paulsen in a dialogue which would have permitted her to explain the selection process. Something tells me this case study has a sequel. More problems were created and no problems were resolved. *(AH)*

DEFINE THE ROLE OF THE VOLUNTEER

Parent volunteers represent one of the most important human resources in the management of a school library media center program. In addition to their valuable assistance in completing many of the routine tasks of library operation, volunteers can also gain an understanding of the impact of the library program on the learning environment. A positive working relationship between the library media specialist and the parent volunteers can result in gaining many adult advocates who will support the library program when special requests are made to the PTO or to the school board.

A clear understanding of the volunteer's role is essential, however, in order to guard against the few volunteers who might use their position to bring undue pressure on changing school policy. The school library media specialist should interview potential volunteers. Included in the interview process should be a list of specific tasks which volunteers would be expected to complete. If there are special talents the volunteer has to offer, then the library media specialist may want to channel such talent to major projects such as organization of book fairs, publishing the library media centers' newsletter, or compiling bibliographies. Such tasks might be reserved for the parent volunteer who has demonstrated that he or she is dependable and trustworthy. *(BNB)*

THE PARENTS' ROLE IN EVALUATION

Certainly there should be the opportunity for parents, and other adults in the community, to voice opinions concerning the quality of materials selected for the school library media center. Such a forum should be clearly separated from the role of the volunteers who assist in the daily operation of the library. Parents may be invited to serve on committees which have been charged with the task of reviewing and selecting materials on potentially controversial topics such as AIDS, child abuse, or nuclear war. When parents are encouraged to work with the librarian, the teachers, and administrators in the preview and review process, time can be given for each party involved to adequately voice opinions about the merits or faults of materials under consideration.

Such direct involvement of parents or other adults of the community in all selection decisions would be cumbersome and would not be a constructive use of time. In 80 to 90 percent of the selection decisions, the professional educator should move to make decisions without such direct community involvement. When selection committees with community membership are established and the educator, either the teacher or the school librarian, takes command of the agenda and establishes a leadership role in facilitating the process, results can be very productive. An end product can be gaining support of parents who have grown in their understanding of the choices educators make in order to obtain quality materials. Should challenges come at some later date, parents who were involved in the preliminary selection process may be valuable defenders of the selection policy followed by the school library media specialist.

The content of collection development policies for most school library media programs is often very sketchy and usually there is a failure to outline in writing the selection process. A section that describes the opportunities others have in voicing opinions concerning instructional materials and the additional resources housed in the library collection is a valuable portion of a collection development policy. More school library media specialists should consider adding such a section to the policy along with procedures concerning what steps will be taken when a formal challenge threatens to remove an item from the collection. Within such policies, the role of the principal and other administrators should be defined as well. Written collection development policies, which have been established with consensus and understanding among administrators, librarians, and board members, should discourage unilateral decisions by any party in the removal of materials from the school library collection. *(DC)*

BIBLIOGRAPHY

Adams, Helen R. *School Media Policy Development: A Practical Process for School Districts.* Littleton, CO: Libraries Unlimited, 1986.
This book deals with many aspects of policy development, but of special interest is the chapter which provides the "argument for policies." Chief among these reasons for policies is to "minimize the outspoken critic of the (school) board's operating procedures and the goals of the school" and to diminish the effect that special interest groups might have on the decision-making policy.

Adult Volunteers: A Handbook for Teacher-Librarians in the Vancouver School Board. Vancouver, BC: Vancouver School Board, 1981, ERIC document 244 625.
This guide for librarians advocates providing volunteers with a handbook to use as an authority as they carry out their duties. Topics covered in the handbook include Goals and Purposes of the Library Resource Center, the Code of Ethics, and the Selection Policy, among others. It is suggested that along with the Selection Policy, procedures for dealing with questioned materials and a list of professional selection aids should be included in the handbook.

American Association of School Librarians and Association for Educational Communications and Technology. *Information Power: Guidelines for School Media Programs.* Chicago: American Library Association, 1988.
See pages 5, 62–64, and 140–48. "Censorship efforts flourish in this time, as they always have. Some individuals and organized groups believe that schools should be purged of books, materials, and courses that contain ideas that conflict with their own convictions."

Bartlett, Larry. "The Iowa Model Policy and Rules for Selection of Instructional Materials." In *Dealing with Censorship.* Edited by James E. Davis, pp. 202–14, Urbana, IL: National Council of Teachers of English, 1979.
This discussion of the Iowa Model Selection Policy spells out the background information of the policy, clarifying specific nontraditional features. Of interest is the section on the Reconsideration Committee. The makeup of the committee departs from the norm by including a *majority of laypeople on the committee,* with a community member as the chairperson. This helps to establish and maintain the committee's credibility with the community. Additionally, the committee meets on a regular basis throughout the school year and not just when a challenge occurs.

Bennett, Linda Leveque. *Volunteers in the School Media Center* Littleton, CO: Libraries Unlimited, 1984.
A useful source for samples of forms which can help communicate the expectations for volunteers. Bennett also describes interview techniques and methods for screening applicants.

Buchanan, William C. "The Principal and the Role Expectations of the Library Media Specialist." *The Clearing House* 55(6) (1982): 253–55.
This article concerns the inaccurate view the principal holds of the role of the library media specialist. The principal does not understand the primary responsibilities of the library media specialist nor does he or she view the librarian as a true colleague. It is up to the library media specialist to educate the principal. The librarian must clarify his or her role as a member of the total instructional team of the school and the one person on the staff who can have the greatest impact on *all* of the children in the school.

Callison, Daniel, and Cynthia Kittleson. "Due Process Principles Applied to the Development of Reconsideration Policies." *Collection Building* 6(4) (1985): 3–9.
Outlines the steps involved in reconsideration of instructional materials in a formal manner. Emphasis is given on the professional role of educators to involve parents and students in both the selection and challenge process. Defines the need for committee work when materials may fall under categories of "innovative," "expensive," or "controversial." Media specialists take a leadership role in establishing such committees.

Hamilton, Donald. "The Principal and the School Library: Their Respective Roles and Common Goals." *Education Canada* 23 (1983):31–38.
This article discusses the fact that few principals are offered training in understanding the role of the school librarian. Hamilton suggests that the librarian, like the principal, has a leadership-management function, and even though the school has a line authority structure, the librarian should operate from a staff authority position when interacting with both the principal and each teacher.

Hopkins, Dianne McAfee. "The School Library Media Specialist: Dealing with Complaints about Materials." *Catholic Library World* 56(3) (1984): 172–74.
This article details how the school library media specialist should handle complaints. First, the media specialist has the primary responsibility for selecting material and should use a school board approved selection policy that includes the following: Objectives of Selection; Responsibility for Selection; Criteria for Selection; Procedures for Selection; and Procedures for Reconsideration of Challenged Materials. The media specialist handles complaints by following the procedures outlined in the selection policy, and the principal is kept informed of developments as they occur.

Jones, Frances M. *Defusing Censorship: The Librarian's Guide to Handling Censorship Conflicts.* Phoenix, AZ: Oryx Press, 1983.
This book concerns censorship in school and public libraries. Of particular interest is the chapter that deals with "responsible planning and effective response." Of primary importance is a written policy for the selection and acquisition of library materials and guidelines concerning who or which positions on the staff are responsible for each step of the process of handling questions, objections, and complaints. Guidelines are

also provided for communicating effectively with individual citizens about their concerns.

Kamhi, Michelle Marder. "Censorship vs. Selection—Choosing the Books Our Children Shall Read." *Educational Leadership* 39(3) (1981): 211–215.

In addition to recommendations for selection and reconsideration of materials, this article discusses the results of a 1980 nationwide survey of selection procedures for library books and classroom texts and challenges to those procedures. The study found that the trend is to include laypeople on state adoption committees; established procedures are vital; there is too much communication with parents that is crisis-oriented; and teaching parents about the books their children read is an effective way to defuse censorship.

Schexnaydre, Linda, and Nancy Burns. *Censorship: A Guide for Successful Workshop Planning.* Phoenix, AZ: Oryx Press. 1984.

This guide outlines workshop sessions including involvement of committees in the reconsideration of materials. Interesting case studies will help one consider many of the issues related to censorship in school libraries.

"Textbook Battles; They're Brewing and Bubbling; By Fall They'll Be Boiling. Don't You Get Scalded." *American School Board Journal* 162(7) (1975): 21–28.

Although this is a somewhat dated article that stemmed from the Kanawa County, West Virginia, 1974–75 textbook controversy, it offers the following valuable advice on preventing differences of opinion about textbooks (and library materials) from becoming full-blown controversies: (1) determine, formulate, legislate, update, and circulate a written selection policy; (2) *involve citizens* in the book selection process; (3) maintain a vigorous public relations program; (4) formulate and write down a policy on how to handle complaints that *allows citizen involvement* in the book re-evaluation process and permits citizens to appeal decisions up the administrative ladder; (5) make sure complaints are in writing; (6) check up on complainants who receive the forms but don't turn them in; and (7) train all "frontline" school personnel in handling book queries and complaints.

Van Orden, Phyllis J. *The Collection Program in Elementary and Secondary Schools: Concepts, Practices, and Information Sources.* Littleton, CO: Libraries Unlimited, 1982.

The chapter on developing policy statements discusses the steps to follow in creating policy statements and provides a sample of the Iowa's "Selection of Instructional Materials: A Model Policy and Rules." In the section on "Objection to Instructional Materials Used," the model suggests that complaints be handled informally whenever possible by the *school official or staff member initially receiving a complaint.* If the issue cannot be resolved informally, then the person raising the question should be referred to *someone designated by the principal* or to the *media specialist.* The main point is that the principal is not necessarily the starting place for handling complaints.

Case 4: Public Library Cooperation

Description

The Laxton County Public Library has completed a plan for future growth based on the guidelines of the American Library Association's publication *A Planning Process*. Although other services will not be cut, areas of future emphasis will be on preschoolers, reference and technical information for local businesses, and the large retired population in the community. Services to secondary schools will receive less attention, as it was felt the public schools have established their own libraries and have a full professional staff of certified school media specialists.

One part of this plan has gone into effect immediately, as the library has stopped its attempt to search for and hire a replacement for the young adult services librarian who retired last month. Instead, this position has been divided so that a new half-time professional position will be added to the two current full-time children's services positions. One half-time reference position can be made full time with emphasis on business information services.

About 6 weeks after these decisions had been made, a phone call was taken by Marsha Fiedler at the Laxton County Junior-Senior High School Media Center.

"For the past two evenings, we have been swamped here at the public library by seventh graders doing reports on folktales and fairy tales. Everything went out with the parents who hit us first, and we've been digging from the encyclopedias since. Most of the kids say the teacher won't allow them to use the encyclopedia. The teacher has not contacted us about the assignment. I seem to remember it from last year. Seems we always have this problem with school assignments. The kids come in masses, along with parents, and they all want the information the night before the paper is due. We don't know when it is going to hit. Last night there seemed to be more high schoolers in here than usual. Have the senior composition papers been assigned?"

The voice of alarm and frustration was that of the head of reference for the public library.

Ms. Fiedler listened, and then replied, "Sorry, I didn't know the folktale assignment had been made. Usually the teacher lets me know, but this year she didn't mention it to me. Seems it usually comes later in the year. As far as the seniors are concerned, the term paper topics have not been assigned. However, we had a biology class in here yesterday and let them know that they may have to use the public library for some materials. I would be surprised if any were ready for the public library as of last night, because the assignment isn't due for 2 weeks."

As the school media specialist:

a. How would you and the reference librarian improve communications?
b. Do you feel you should have any input concerning the direction of the public library and its future planning?
c. What are the responsibilities of the teacher and of the media specialist in making the public library aware of assignments with high demand from many students for few materials?

Response

KEEP A CALENDAR

Ideally teachers and school librarians would notify the public library of any mass assignments. In actuality, this seldom happens. Teachers often give assignments for which they have not checked to see whether materials are available to meet the reading levels and numbers of students who will be doing the assignments. The lack of communication from teachers is easy to understand when one considers their teaching days are filled to capacity. Teachers seldom think a library will not be able to meet an informational need.

It is the media specialist's role to foster communication with her faculty and to encourage them to let her and the public librarian know whenever library assignments are being given. Also, both types of librarians can keep a calendar from year to year, noting when certain types of assignments are given. This calendar can serve as an informal guideline for future planning. *(MMJ)*

COMMUNICATE WITH YOUR STAFF AND BEYOND

Cooperation, coordination, and communication are missing fundamental elements of library service in Laxton County. The resulting problems and poor quality of service to young adults are the unfortunate consequences of this practice. Communication must be established before the higher goals of cooperation and ultimately coordination of services can be reached. The breakdown in communication did not start with the retirement of the YA services librarian. The head of reference states, "We always have this problem with school assignments." Lines of communication had not existed between the YA librarian and the school librarian, who would have otherwise contacted the public library about the biology assignment. In addition, the YA librarian apparently had not made her role visible to the school librarian, her colleagues, or her administration—some of whom might have fought to have the position spared.

The head of reference is justifiably frustrated and yet he always has this problem. He remembers the assignment from last year, but he hasn't worked with the past YA librarian to develop any solutions. He hasn't even talked with the two children's librarians on his own staff to seek help with the folktale assignment. Did he even think of their resources?

Ms. Fiedler has not communicated well with her teaching colleagues or the public library. She was not aware of the folktale assignment although she did know about the senior term papers. She even recommended the public library to biology students but failed to notify the public library of the assignment or of its 2-week due date.

Communication needs to improve immediately. To begin, a meeting of Ms. Fiedler, the head of reference, and at least one of the children's librarians must occur. Including a teacher would be beneficial since helping students research assignments is the immediate goal. Assignment alert and teacher notification forms are used by many public and school libraries with varying degrees of success (see figures 4 and 5 for a sample assignment alert and a sample teacher notification form). This initial meeting could result in the production of such forms and in future plans for opening the lines of communication.

Ms. Fiedler should inform the teachers of her desire to improve reference service to their students and ask for teacher input. Assignment alerts, copies of teachers' recommended reading lists, and a copy of the curriculum should be shared with the public library. Ms. Fiedler could invite the public librarians to speak at a staff meeting and to visit the school library and classrooms.

The adult reference and children's librarians need to work together to handle class assignments efficiently. Phone calls to teachers

Figure 4. Sample Assignment Alert

OAK LAWN
PUBLIC LIBRARY
9427 S. RAYMOND AVENUE ● OAK LAWN, ILLINOIS 60453 ● (312)422-4993

ASSIGNMENT   ALERT

Please send at least one week prior to assignment.

Length of assignment/dates: from_____ to_____

School_____Phone_____Teacher_____

Name of course_____No. of students_____Grade(s)_____

Assignment: (Please be as specific as possible. A copy of the assignment is helpful.)

Purpose of the assignment:

____ Practice using library materials   ____ Information gathering with as
with only normal librarian   much special attention as can be
assistance.   provided by the Library.

Do you desire materials pertinent to the assignment to be held for Library use only?

____ Yes   ____ No

Type(s) of library materials students will probably seek to meet this assignment:

____ Reference   ____ Pamphlets   ____ Periodicals

____ Fiction   ____ Non-fiction   ____ A-V Materials

Additional information to aid the librarians:

Reprinted with permission from Oak Lawn Public Library, Oak Lawn, IL.

Figure 5. Sample Teacher Notification Form

**OAK LAWN
PUBLIC LIBRARY**
9427 S. RAYMOND AVENUE ● OAK LAWN, ILLINOIS 60453 ● (312)422-4993

TEACHER NOTIFICATION FORM

Oak Lawn Public Library
9427 Raymond Avenue
Oak Lawn, IL 60453
422-4990   Date_____

(Teacher)   (School)

_____ came to the Library today. We were

unable to fill the request for _____

because:

_____ All material on this topic is in use.

_____ Too many limitations have been placed on types of materials to be used.

_____ Material on this subject is in the "Reference" collection and cannot
be checked out.

_____ Further explanation of the question is needed.

_____ Careful search failed to supply useful materials.

_____ We are unable to supply so much information on one topic to so many students
at once.

_____ Information on this topic is being used by Library patrons not in your class.

_____ Other_____

_____

We request that you give us advance notice of your assignments if possible so
that we may serve your students better. We welcome a visit from you.

Department_____   Librarian_____

Reprinted with permission from Oak Lawn Public Library, Oak Lawn, IL.

or the school librarian should be made freely to clarify the assignments if needed. The librarians could develop a brochure describing school services provided by the public library.

Once the librarians in Laxton County begin communicating they can advance to active cooperation and coordination of services. Possibilities for cooperation abound: programming, collection development, union lists, shared expensive resources, and mutual support during times of crisis. *(CKD)*

BIBLIOGRAPHY

Aaron, Shirley L. "School/Public Library Cooperation: The Way It Is." *Catholic Library World* 52(7) (1981): 280–85.
Shirley Aaron has written extensively concerning school and public library cooperation. Her article focuses on "the current interest in school/public library cooperation, the content of recent research, an examination of the components of cooperative activities, and a discussion of outstanding examples of cooperative programs."

American Association of School Librarians and Association for Educational Communications and Technology. *Information Power: Guidelines for School Library Media Programs.* Chicago: American Library Association, 1988.
See pages 12–13. "Often library media specialists do not have the planning time necessary to effectively participate in resource sharing."

Black, Nancy, Ken Roberts, and Valerie White. "School Assignments: A Public Library Responsibility." *Emergency Librarian* 13(5) (1986): 25–26.
Gives examples of how public libraries and school libraries can share responsibilities for both curriculum support and student personal reading.

Fitzgibbons, Shirley. "Research on Library Services for Children and Young Adults: Implications for Practice." In *Kids and Libraries.* Edited by Ken Haycock and Carol-Ann Haycock, pp. 51–62. Seattle, WA: Dyad Services, 1984.
This is a comprehensive review of research concerning library programs for children. Most of the studies examined are from the mid-1960s to the early 1980s. "Use and User Studies," "Reading Motivation," "School/Public Library Cooperation," and "Services to Special Groups" are covered.

Morning, Todd, and Janet Watkins. "Beyond Assignment Alert." *Illinois Libraries* 67(1) (1985): 37–39.
Teacher packets, newsletters, and other forms of written correspondence are described.

Roeder, Joan. "School/Public Library Cooperation: A View from the School Yard." *Illinois Libraries* 65(7) (1983): 452–54
A list of ideas and activities which could lead to cooperation.

School Media Quarterly 7(1) (1978).
A special issue of *SMQ* devoted to the joint role of the school and public library in community education. Shirley L. Aaron and Lois D. Fleming provide constructive conclusions based on several major studies.

Sullivan, Peggy. "Library Cooperation to Serve Youth." In *Libraries and Young Adults: Media, Services, and Librarianship.* Edited by JoAnn V. Rogers, pp. 113-18. Littleton, CO: Libraries Unlimited, 1979.
Sullivan addresses several areas in which cooperation is needed, but often not considered. Public libraries need to cooperate with private schools as well as public schools and also consider special services which might be provided to children who are not in school. She also warns large libraries and large school districts not to become so involved in grand formal planning that day-to-day services to youth become less effective.

White, Brenda H., ed. "Collection Management for School Library Media Centers." *Collection Management* 7(3/4) (1985–86).
This special issue devoted to collection development problems in school media programs has one section concerning cooperation between public and school libraries. Of importance for this case are the following articles: "The Use of School Libraries and Public Libraries and the Relationship to Collection Development," by Blanche Woolls, 173–82; "School and Public Library Cooperation: A Prerequisite for Cooperative Collection Development," by Betty V. Billman and Patricia Owens, 183–96; and "Cooperative Materials Purchasing among School and Public Libraries," by Mary Ellen Kennedy, 197–204.

Woolls, Blanche. "Cooperative Library Services between Public Libraries and School Libraries." In *School Library Media Centers: Research Studies and the State-of-the-Art.* Edited by David V. Loertscher. ERIC Clearinghouse of Information Resources, pp. 41–54. Syracuse, NY: Syracuse University, 1980.
Three major studies are summarized. Major conclusions include (1) professional librarians must actively seek cooperation—it is not a natural event; (2) there is limited contact between school and public librarians through professional organizations; and (3) successful programs demand time and long-range planning.

Case 5: Credit for Student Library Assistant

Description

Following several national studies and position statements, the state legislature approved legislation that calls for secondary school students to be in a class for academic credit at least 6 hours each school day. The curriculum committee for the White County Community Schools has taken action based on that legislation and its members' interpretation of the same national warnings concerning weaknesses in public education. No longer will half credits be awarded for student assistants who enroll as teacher aides or library media center aides.

None of the school media specialists serves on the current district curriculum committee, although they have been represented in the past.

Jean Marshall, head media specialist for the single high school in the district, had developed a large crew of student assistants. Her program included at least four student assistants each hour. Tasks included delivery of equipment, operation and minor maintenance of equipment, circulation duties for both book and periodical check-out and check-in, and shelving of materials. Several of the students have been "helpers" in the library since their sophomore year, and Ms. Marshall usually encouraged these more experienced students to tutor fellow students on basic or introductory skills in using the library. Peer tutoring was common for helping slower students use periodical indexes and locate reference materials. Only two seniors had been used as peer tutors before, but things seemed to work well. Ms. Marshall wanted eventually to have several students available in the media center to tutor other students in basic computer language skills. It seemed a natural setting for this to take place in the media center, and Ms. Marshall had read in recent educational literature evidence that peer instruction tended to help many students become acquainted with microcomputer operations and programming skills.

In addition, Ms. Marshall and the head of the business department had designed a program to allow for full credit to be granted to students who work as student secretaries. These students would work one hour each school day and complete written correspondence, print out overdue notices, and handle some of the routine cataloging tasks. Ms. Marshall had observed how well a similar program had worked at another high school.

Ms. Marshall had never tested her student assistants concerning knowledge of information location skills and the general operation of the library, but she was willing to do so.

As the option for credit closed, Ms. Marshall feared she might lose as many as half of her student aides. Lacking an assistant, and having only one full-time clerk, she felt such a loss would cause great problems in providing the level of service established in the past.

As Ms. Marshall, consider the following questions:

a. What might be done to have more input in the decisions of the curriculum committee?
b. What can be done to show that student assistance in the library is worth academic credit?
c. Are the peer-tutoring and student secretary positions really worth the trouble?
d. How might a library assistant be tested in order to demonstrate he or she should receive academic credit?

Response

The basic problem is the lack of written objectives concerning the instruction being given, no evaluation of the students, and no recognition of the value of student assistants to maintain the level of service expected by teachers.

SHOW RATIONALE FOR ACADEMIC CREDIT

Show the curriculum committee that the program of instruction these student assistants receive, and the services they provide, are as important to their overall education as the information they are learning in other curriculum areas.

The first step would be to get your objectives in writing. This shows you are doing something with instruction. One objective might be: To provide students with marketable skills. The Roberts article in *School Library Journal,* May 1985 (see bibliography), stated that utilizing students as helpers in a school media center not only provides much needed assistance in the media center, but also offers students much needed work experience.

Students who worked in the media center of Our Lady of the Elms High School received special consideration when they applied for jobs in the community because employers were aware of the diverse library media instruction skills and the on-the-job training these student assistants received.

Develop a written curriculum for the student assistants to use as a course syllabus. The academic value can be used to make your case with the committee. *(KSB)*

EVALUATE STUDENT HELPERS

Montgomery Catholic High School in Alabama used the grade contract method of evaluation. An example of their contract was that for a grade of "C," students must turn in weekly an activity report documenting their performance of "regular" and "rotating" duties along with any "other" assigned duties. For a "B," students submit the same report, and once a quarter they must prepare a bulletin board accompanied by a display of books that relates to their bulletin board and prepare one book review. To receive an "A," they turn in the weekly report, do a bulletin board/display, and prepare two written book reviews, and they must obtain one book review from a fellow student who is not a library assistant. Students in Osgood, Indiana, earn a credit in English for a course called "Library Science." During the first semester these students review reference materials; during the second semester they learn a barrage of machine operations. They too turn in a daily duty sheet showing the tasks accomplished (see Figure 6 for a sample duty sheet). *(JJ)*

SHOW STATISTICAL EVIDENCE

Keep statistics that will show how students receiving academic credit are tested. Keep records of:

1. Number of students showing AV presentations in classes
2. Number of contacts with teachers and students
3. Kinds of tasks students help with, so that the librarian is free of mundane chores
4. Number of repairs done by students, and the money and time saved by their doing the repairs
5. The written and practical tests on pieces of equipment, their operation, and their maintenance

These records should be part of the student's evaluation in the written course. *(MLS)*

Figure 6. Sample Student Librarian Duty Sheet

DAILY WORKSHEET
LIBRARY SERVICE

To make sure that all student librarians are carrying their share of the work load, this check sheet has been devised. The sheet is to be used at the end of every period and failure to do so will result in no points for the day. (CREDIT STUDENTS MUST COMPLETE THE SHEET AS PART OF THEIR GRADE.)

A total of 15 points per day will be considered as a perfect score. All entries are 1 point unless noted.

	Mon.	Tues.	Wed.	Thurs.	Fri.
Logged times for exits (at least 10)	___	___	___	___	___
Logged ingoing students (at least 10)	___	___	___	___	___
Checked out any book	___	___	___	___	___
Ran a search on the computer (at least 5)	___	___	___	___	___
Carded returned books (at least 5)	___	___	___	___	___
Shelved books from the truck (at least 10)	___	___	___	___	___
Deleted books from the computer (at least 3)	___	___	___	___	___
Entered titles on the computer (at least 5)	___	___	___	___	___
Straightened chairs	___	___	___	___	___
Straightened magazines (at the end of each period)	___	___	___	___	___
Retrieved magazines from stacks (at least 3)	___	___	___	___	___
Helped a student in research	___	___	___	___	___
Did Homework (3 points)	___	___	___	___	___
Straightened shelves (at least 2)	___	___	___	___	___
Straightened paperbacks	___	___	___	___	___
Ran an errand for the Librarian (point for each errand)	___	___	___	___	___
Checked in mail, newspapers, etc.	___	___	___	___	___
Colored or cut display items	___	___	___	___	___
Typed a new card	___	___	___	___	___
Cleaned (desk drawer, tables, floors, etc.)	___	___	___	___	___
Filed magazines (3 pts.) (at least 5)	___	___	___	___	___
Reported any of these offenders (1 for each offense)	___	___	___	___	___
2 Recs - no more					
Rec doing reference					
Overdue or fines					
More than 2 minutes in the hall					
Checked out materials for faculty	___	___	___	___	___
Checked in faculty materials	___	___	___	___	___
DAILY TOTALS	___	___	___	___	___

Reprinted with permission from *Indiana Media Journal,* designed by Freda Jo Kegley, Jac-Cen-Del School Corporation, Osgood, IN.

EMPHASIZE SERVICES STUDENT HELPERS PROVIDE

It may be necessary to show that services provided with student helpers, such as peer tutoring and programs operated in conjunction with other faculty members, will have to be deleted because of lack of help. A dynamic library program would be impossible to continue without student helpers. Everyone gains with student helpers.

Since there is evidence in educational literature to support peer instruction, it would seem a worthwhile project to pilot. *(KSB)*

DOCUMENT STUDENT PROGRESS

It may be too late to save Ms. Marshall's program for this year. The lack of representation on the curriculum committee may be fatal. Only a concerted effort may restore the lost assistants for the coming year. Convince this group of what will be missing from the library media program.

It is vital for anyone using student assistants to have a formal, organized program with tests to evaluate students' progress. This curriculum guide is necessary to receive approval from other teachers. It enables them to recognize library media skills as a body of knowledge. They can see how being a student assistant provides worthwhile learning experiences. Ms. Marshall's students have acquired valuable skills and attitudes about knowledge, information, communication, and people that will last a lifetime. Now she must bring this to the attention of the district curriculum committee. *(JM)*

SEVERAL LEVELS FOR STUDENT ASSISTANTS

The school media specialist should keep in mind that there are several possible "levels" of student assistants. In some cases, students will volunteer and perform tasks without receiving credit. The administration should know what criteria these students meet. Perhaps these are students who come to the library on "free time" and shelve books or dust shelves. The tasks of these students should be made clearly different from those of students who meet entry-level criteria (word processing skills, basic knowledge of library operations) and then provide regular productive services.

The media specialist may want to consider providing the opportunity for the student library media assistant to train other classroom teacher assistants. This provides a model for teaching others important library or media use skills and relates to the media specialist's professional role of teaching fellow teachers the potential for new materials and equipment.

The highest-level student assistant at the senior high school level is the student who performs several important independent tasks. These might include the following:

1. Senior high school students could offer storytelling and assist in helping with reading skills by traveling to elementary school libraries or by helping in special education classes.
2. The business department may be willing to cooperate in the development of a student secretary program in which senior high school students perform important secretarial duties in exchange for letters of reference and credit through the business department.
3. Many senior high students are capable of teaching basic reference and search skills to fellow students. This role may be especially important as more and more schools use online searching. Students experienced in such searching techniques can provide valuable assistance, and they should receive credit for their expertise. *(JK)*

BIBLIOGRAPHY

American Association of School Librarians and Association for Educational Communications and Technology. *Information Power: Guidelines for School Library Media Programs.* Chicago: American Library Association, 1988.
See pages 62–64. "These students can be valuable assets whose volunteer efforts contribute significantly to the library media program. They, in return, may receive valuable social, developmental, and educational experiences."

Bard, Therese Bissen. "Menehunes in the Library." *School Library Journal* (1983): 17–19.
An elementary school library uses student assistants in a dynamic program. The article summarizes the experiences with organizing and training student assistants and also offers helpful suggestions on how to work with student helpers. Seven objectives are listed that clearly describe what students are expected to gain by working in the library—objectives have no age limit—very appropriate for any age. Tells how assistants are selected, their duties, how they're taught, and how to find them. The "incentives and rewards" section discussed at the end is age-related, but the article has excellent information and could easily be utilized in a high school setting.

Elliot, Mark, and Nyla Leonard. "Upgraded Library Skills Needed by Office Personnel." *Business Education Forum* (1988): 17–19.
A reference librarian and an instructor in office occupations at a small community college implement a unit in an existing course, Office Reference Materials, to increase the research and library skills of office workers. The objectives were to introduce students to materials relating to office or secretarial concerns—for example, *Encyclopedia of Associations,*

Robert's Rules of Order, and many others. A sample worksheet is included for one of the materials and several objectives are listed at the end of the unit evaluation. "Hands-on" use of the card catalogue (L.C. & D.D.C.), *Magazine Index, Readers' Guide,* and several others are also demonstrated.

Hedin, Diane. "Students as Teachers: A Tool for Improving School Climate and "Productivity." *Social Policy* 17(3) (1987): 42–47.
A thoroughly comprehensive report of the values of peer-tutoring and cross age tutoring. Several instances are listed in which they have proven effective. Benefits are listed and described, both for the tutor and the tutee. The tutor, for example, assumes a new, responsible role as a teacher and heightens his or her sense of competence and adequacy. The tutee has an individualized learning experience and can improve academic performance. Note that about 8% of public schools offer credit for community service, which tutoring qualifies as, but hopes for more in the future.

Kegley, Freda Jo. "English Credit for Student Librarians." *Indiana Media Journal* 8(1) (1985): 9–12.
Students can earn credit provided they meet certain criteria established by the school librarian. Students must meet high expectations in reference skills, equipment operation, media production, and general clerical tasks.

Lander, Faye. "Aides Acquire Marketable Skills." *School Library Journal* 29(10) (1983): 34.
The media specialist of an Akron, Ohio, high school offers work experience, specific skills, and good references—plus opportunity to receive credit for these services. Part of the training is to have students instruct each other. Students see the operation of 11 types of machines and learn how to operate them. They are exposed to demonstrations of online searches and public library services such as *Magazine Index.* After instruction, students are recruited to work in the media center. Several different duties are listed and explained. Community members report that these students receive special consideration when applying for paying jobs after high school.

Roberts, Beverly J., and Isabel Schon. "Student Aides in Arizona School Libraries: A Descriptive Study." *School Library Journal* 31(9) (1985): 32–35.
Reports on a questionnaire survey sent to 170 Arizona elementary school librarians to determine if students are being used as aides and the extent of their involvement in library media programs.

Case 6: A Standard Style Manual

Description

For the past 3 years at Jefferson High School, the two full-time media specialists have been working to expand the research paper demands for the social studies, science, and English departments. For the most part, this effort has been successful. The number of reports is up. Several teachers not involved in the use of library resources before have become interested and have been designing library research units.

One problem has remained. There seems to be no common style for citations which all of the teachers accept. Some require footnoting, and some do not require any citation for sources at all. Some refuse to allow students to use encyclopedic information, while others see encyclopedias as sources for good beginning background material. None of the teachers has accepted the idea that nonprint materials or interviews can be used to document the evidence presented in a report.

Even within the English department no consistent requirements are given for documentation of references in a composition. Within the five senior English classes, three different style manuals are used.

The head of the English department is interested in finding some standard for the entire school, but the head of the social studies department and the head of the science department have no interest in the matter.

As the school media specialist, consider the following:

a. Should there be an attempt to standardize the format for research reports and papers?
b. If a standard is to be found, who should take the lead?
c. What is the role of the media specialist?

Response

UNIFORMITY WITH FLEXIBILITY

A major responsibility of the media specialist is to implement the educational program by working directly with teachers to facilitate and expedite their teaching and by working directly with students to enhance their learning. In the case being studied here, the absence of a uniform style manual seriously hinders the efforts of the English teachers to instruct students on the preparation of research papers and most definitely jeopardizes the students' learning of this process. Just as science students are taught consistent steps to follow in scientific experimentation, so English students should be taught consistent steps in preparing research papers—and these steps should be adopted throughout the school.

The media specialist has the unique position that provides a link between teachers on an interdisciplinary level and affords a view of students' overall curricular requirements. A committee should be formed consisting of the library media specialist, chairperson of the English department, and one to three other faculty members (depending on the number available and expressing an interest). This committee should first survey the faculty members who currently assign research papers as to their requirements in terms of style. Some consistencies may appear that are not evident by casual observance. The committee should then have the authority to prepare a style manual that maintains certain standards of quality and is consistent with the overall needs of the faculty and students. Care should be taken that the manual not be overly confining. For example, either footnotes or endnotes should be acceptable, but citations should be required and the format of those should be consistent. Likewise, types of reference materials allowed should be left to the teacher's discretion—an encyclopedia may not be acceptable for a college prep student's research paper in English but might be the perfect choice for a two-page freshman report on a historical topic.

The committee might also want to consider the possibility of "team-grading" of research papers. The English teachers and/or media specialist might offer to grade *all* research papers in the school solely on the basis of style—though this sounds cumbersome, it really does not take long to check footnotes, bibliographies, and other basic style elements. In return, the social studies and science teachers would agree to read research papers prepared for English classes that deal with topics related to social studies or science and grade them for content. One should not expect teachers outside of the English department to have the expertise or the time to grade on style-related matters. Yet if no attention is given to the style manual being followed, the situation will quickly return to the current one. *(JP)*

BIBLIOGRAPHY

Several common standard guides for secondary school students are:

Bailey, Edward P., Philip A. Powell, and Jack M. Shuttleworth. *Writing Research Papers: A Practical Guide.* New York: Holt, Rinehart and Winston, 1981.

Gibaldi, Joseph, and Walter S. Achtert, eds. *MLA Handbook* (student edition). 2nd ed. New York: Modern Language Association, 1984.

Gorden, Charlotte. *How to Find What You Want in the Library.* Barron's Educational Series, 1978.

Hubbuch, Susan M. *Writing Research Papers across the Curriculum.* New York: Holt, Rinehart and Winston, 1985.

Katz, William. *Your Library: A Reference Guide.* 2nd ed. New York: Holt, Rinehart and Winston, 1984.

Kuhlthau, Carol Collier. *Teaching the Library Research Process: A Step by Step Program for Secondary School Students.* Center for Applied Research in Education, 1985.
Although this book is not a style manual, Kuhlthau's advice and recommendations are essential to a successful term paper project on the secondary school level.

Meyer, Michael. *The Little, Brown Guide to Writing Research Papers.* Boston: Little, Brown and Company, 1985.

Turabian, Kate L. *A Manual for Writers of Term Papers.* 5th ed. Chicago: University of Chicago Press, 1987.

Case 7: Countering the Teacher Planning Period

Description

Wilma Burns is ready to begin her second year as the full-time school media specialist at Eastwood Elementary. Last year she tolerated a schedule that had been established by the previous media specialist, who had served for 18 years.

Under the current routine, each teacher receives six one-hour planning periods each week. These periods are covered by the school's music teacher, art teacher, and media specialist. The art teacher and the music teacher each visit the classroom for one hour two times a week. Each visit, the teacher sends the students to the media center for reading, storytelling from the media specialist, or any kind of practice in library skills the media specialist wants to try. The teacher is not required to attend. As a matter of fact, most teachers stay only long enough to drop the kids off and then pick them up.

The teachers have never attempted to become involved in what was being taught so that the library skills could be reinforced in the classroom or in future planned visits to the library.

Ms. Burns felt a great deal of frustration with the routine. She had been involved in a media program in her previous school in which teachers planned programs with the media specialist and scheduled the students to use the library. Under that approach Ms. Burns could prepare for specific skills which had been identified by the teacher and herself working as a team.

Ms. Burns has mentioned to the principal several problems the current routine causes:

1. Teachers feel no need to develop library units beyond the routine visits because they think enough time has been given to library skills with the two hours each week.
2. Students tend to see some visits as pointless when they are required to go to the library twice a week whether they need to or not.

3. There is no attempt by the teacher to build on the library skills the students have been taught.
4. There is no time for the media specialist to plan since she is scheduled completely from one day to the next to cover these classes.

The principal seems to agree, but feels the art and music teachers "pull it off" without any problems, and besides, the classroom teachers have grown fond of the planning periods. They don't expect or want a change.

Consider the following questions in Ms. Burn's situation:

a. Do her arguments have merit? Could she do more with the students under the current routine?
b. If Ms. Burns wants a change, where does she begin, and what steps should be taken?

Response

SHARE EXAMPLES OF SUCCESSFUL PLANNING

In scheduling released time librarians are unfortunately lumped with art, music, and physical education at the elementary level. The big difference lies in job requirements. Whereas the music, art, and physical education teachers are hired to teach, the librarian is hired to teach, to administer the library, and to provide necessary resources for teachers and students. If all the specialists are treated uniformly, that makes the librarian a full-time teacher of library/reference skills and literature; there is no time to do the rest of the job.

The case states that Ms. Burns has spoken to her principal but the principal is reluctant to act. Ms. Burns must place her emphasis on doing what is best educationally for the students and build a convincing argument that the school will receive more from the professional library/media professional with less scheduled time. If the school can provide a better instructional program for the students, how can changes take place to bring that about? Few administrators will fight your objective to better the students' educational environment. What Ms. Burns needs to encourage (and perhaps draft herself) are specific goals and dates by which changes will occur.

Ms. Burns says she had experience at a school where teachers planned with her. She should share specific examples of how this worked both with the principal and with teachers she feels might be receptive. *(MPD)*

NO INNOVATION WITHOUT FLEXIBLE TIME PLANNING

This case is not unusual and is a major problem for elementary school library/media specialists. If one is scheduled too tightly, no extra services are ever implemented because there is simply no time, and the professional's morale is low as he or she is used as a baby-sitter. When no extra resourcing is done, no special programs are developed, and no interdisciplinary units carried out, then staff and administration see no reason to change the library schedule. It can be a circular problem, and it takes those with assertiveness and confidence in their ability to build a superior program to convince entrenched staff members and administrators to break away. However, it *can* be done and *must* be done if we are truly to provide professional services at this level. *(MPD)*

A VICTIM OF STATE LAWS

Ms. Burns, along with many other elementary librarians, is victimized by state laws and/or local traditional patterns that recognize the need for planning time for classroom teachers but do not provide appropriate personnel to accommodate the released time for teachers. School librarians become convenient and vulnerable targets for exploitation.

At least the principal agrees with Ms. Burns; however, has she or he requested funds to hire a "floating" teacher to provide the needed released time? Music and art teachers do not generally have daily responsibilities beyond those of the classroom; the library media specialist has a full-time job in addition to classroom teaching.

If Ms. Burns does not have a position description that reflects the library responsibilities of a school library media specialist, this might be a reasonable beginning point, preferably as a joint effort by the librarian and the principal. Ms. Burns and the principal need to explore alternatives that will permit the optimal use of Ms. Burns's time and recognize the librarian's unique educational role. Since Ms. Burns functioned successfully as a team member in the past, she has much to offer the school in terms of improving the learning environment for students and the teaching environment for teachers. Ms. Burns might investigate and share some of the studies that indicate the greater effectiveness of teaching library skills in context rather than in isolation. She might also visit with elementary school librarians who have received awards for outstanding programs and relay their success stories to the principal.

Ms. Burns might become active in her state professional organizations and work with a group of colleagues in attempts to address this issue at the state level. Legislative bodies and policy-making groups on all levels need to become more informed about the students' denial of access to library materials and facilities when librarians are not permitted to function in their professional roles. *(AH)*

MEDIA CENTERS SHOULD BE OPEN TO ALL

The media center isn't just the librarian's domain; it's everybody's place, open to everyone, *whenever* anyone needs to use it. This is not possible in Ms. Burns' library because she has a full schedule, except, of course, during her personal released time.

Students should spend more time in the school library media center to learn and practice information skills *coordinated* with class work and should be tested for competency in information skills in English, math, science, social studies, and computer science.

Ms. Burns should cite examples and reiterate the success of the media program in her previous school in which teachers planned programs with the media specialist and scheduled the students to use the library. She also needs to help the principal realize that librarians have (1) a commitment to the welfare of the entire media center, (2) access to a vast amount of information, and (3) knowledge to share about the technology of our times.

Ms. Burns will have the students for 2 hours, which is a lot of time that should not go to waste. She might develop some listening centers and work/research stations that would stimulate interest, add variety, and support recreational reading. She could have some reading contests. She might have students develop a newspaper, thereby being able to include not only their creative efforts but some "PR" to support her need to be off the release time schedule. She could develop a program for fifth and sixth graders to become library volunteers, relieving her of some of the clerical duties. However, the problem with these ideas is that they take time to accomplish and she has a full schedule already.

Ms. Burns might negotiate to have a substitute hired occasionally so she can have time to discuss and plan with teachers for more meaningful activities that can carry over from the media center to the classroom even if the teachers do not stay. Eventually they might see the benefits that this type of activity is sure to bring about and be open to other ways of securing their released time. She could also visit classrooms and provide materials for special teaching units or do book talks if the system would agree to hiring a substitute. *(AW)*

BIBLIOGRAPHY

American Association of School Librarians and Association for Educational Communications and Technology. *Information Power: Guidelines for School Library Media Programs.* Chicago: American Library Association, 1988.
See pages 27–39. "Class visits to the library media center are scheduled to facilitate use at the point of need. Any functions that restrict or interfere with open access to all resources, including scheduled classes on a fixed basis, must be avoided to the fullest extent possible."

Haycock, Carol-Ann. "Developing the School Resource Centre Program: A Systematic Approach." *Emergency Librarian* 12(1) (1984): 9–16.
This plan is complete with sample forms and a scheduling format. Effort given to follow this plan can lead to more cooperation between the librarian and the teacher.

School Media Quarterly. 4(3) (1976).
This special issue of the *SMQ* provides some of the important thoughts from several experts who were beginning to formulate the instructional role of the school media specialist. Team teaching and curriculum development are discussed as essential roles for the school librarian.

Case 8: Critical Thinking Skills

Description

For the past 8 years Steven Malcolm has been successful, he feels, in developing a program for students to learn the basic skills for using the library. Each sophomore at his high school is required to pass a test which involves the use of the card catalog and the basic periodical indexes. There is a library skills curriculum which has been in place for grades 3–12 for several years. From elementary grades through the senior class, students become acquainted with the common reference tools available through the school library.

There seems to be a need for more, however. Mr. Malcolm believes that students often use just any material they can locate without considering its merits or problems. There seems to be no concern on the part of many teachers that students do not seek out evidence to support arguments and materials which present both sides of a question. The basic approach is to make the use of the library as "cut and dry" as possible. "Learn to locate materials so you can get the assignment done." "Don't question the quality of the materials." "Feel satisfied if you can find enough to meet the minimum requirements." "Contacting other libraries for more extensive information is not worth the time and expense."

Mr. Malcolm knows the development of the library skills program has been hard work, and both he and his teachers feel they have established more library-related assignments than the average high school. To establish a program that expects students to be critical in the use of information seems beyond the expectations of the teachers. But Mr. Malcolm knows there is room for improvement, even if he has to take on the design of the critical lesson plans without help from others.

As Mr. Malcolm, consider the following:

   a. What are critical thinking skills and how do they relate to the use of the library?

    b. Should the librarian take the responsibility for designing units of study that are outside the set curriculum?

    c. In what ways can Mr. Malcolm begin to introduce the more specialized and demanding use of materials?

    d. Can he justify requests for more money in order to use the interlibrary loan program, or acquire materials that support lessons on critical thinking skills lessons when there is no current teacher support?

Response

TEACHING STUDENTS TO THINK

A 1961 statement of the National Education Association referred to American education and stated that the "purpose which runs through and strengthens all other educational purposes...is the development of the ability to think." As our society moves further into the information age, the seriousness of this purpose becomes even more evident. Not only do educators have a responsibility to teach students to think, but they must also teach them to think critically. This means to evaluate both print and oral information and decide its merits on the basis of the author's or speaker's qualifications, the bias of the information, the point of view presented, and the accuracy of the information. As future citizens, students must realize that just because something is written in a book, magazine, or newspaper or is seen on television it may not be factual or present the only valid viewpoint. The media specialist has a unique role and responsibility in this process. A joint AASL and AECT standards statement released in 1975 declares the *major* purpose of the school library media program to be to improve the educational experience of the students by building "bridges between content and context, purpose and procedure." Other documents prepared by both professional library and education organizations concur with the philosophy that the school library media program should be an integral part of the total learning environment and the media specialist should have a role in curriculum development, serving as the vital link between the teacher and classroom materials or other resources. *(JP)*

SUPPORT FROM TEACHERS

A brief review of literature on education offers little help in defining the concept of critical thinking skills. Many definitions suggest that the act of problem solving requires the student to make a "mental leap" of logic that defies quantitative investigation.

Should the librarian take the responsibility of designing units of study that are outside the set curriculum? As a general response, the answer is no. However, improvements in the library skills curriculum with the help of a sympathetic teacher would be feasible.

If an improved program succeeds on a pilot basis, then it can be expanded to other areas if given support by teachers and administrators. A pilot program can be used to introduce the more demanding and specialized use of materials. Some aspects of this program could be determining author bias or the value of primary versus secondary sources.

The media specialist cannot justify requests for more money to use interlibrary loan or materials for critical thinking when there is no teacher support. The "greatest" program in the world will fail if there is no audience. You cannot give away something that no one wants. However, if the pilot project is slowly nurtured to gain support and an audience, then the request for more funding can be made. At that point, the request would have a much better chance for success. *(JAB)*

INTEGRATE LIBRARY SKILLS

All programs within an educational institution are most effective when they are coordinated and integrated to include as many curricular areas as possible.

Library instruction with purpose, direction, and application is far more effective than instruction in isolation of the school curriculum. It readily demonstrates the philosophy that the library is not only a storehouse of information but the facility that can provide avenues of opportunity for individualized instruction and professional assistance in locating and assimilating information to meet specific needs.

Critical thinking skills are techniques that a student develops, correlating basic educational skills with decision-making skills to make the best choice in light of all the information available. In this situation, informational retrieval skills are also integrated into the process.

Refining the processes of critical selection and implementation can begin as early as students start using the library. Deciding what material best fits the need, assuming responsibility for care of materials, returning borrowed items, making selections from a variety of choices, exploring alternatives, and discussing the consequences of choices can be integrated into even the early stages of the program.

Higher degrees of performance can be integrated at various levels appropriate to the age group and ability level of students. A sequential plan of skill achievement should be established with the cooperation of colleagues to provide research skills appropriate for job expectations and the degree of proficiency necessary to achieve quality performance. Teachers really do desire that their students achieve maximum potential. If Mr. Malcolm approaches the problem as a concern for students to achieve a higher quality of performance to meet teacher expectations, renewed support and cooperation should be generated.

Administrators generally solicit concrete evidence on which to base additional funding requests for program expansion. A reevaluation of the present program, a unified approach for student performance, and a sequentially integrated research/critical thinking skills program would certainly strengthen the need for such a request. Positive results would lend even greater support. *(AR)*

GIVE STUDENTS TIME TO THINK

The introduction of critical thinking skills requires that the school librarian consider the information needs of the student beyond those which the teacher or librarian may feel all students have. Information needs cannot usually be determined until the student begins to raise questions and search for answers. Time and assistance are needed for both exercises. Sessions in "What is a good question?" and "What is a good information source?" are more valuable than treasure hunts for meaningless facts and figures. In order for critical thinking skills to be integrated into information selection and use skills, the school librarian must:

1. After using trivial information exercises in order to get students acquainted with several reference sources, move beyond such exercises quickly. "Treasure hunts" are often seen by students as busy work.

2. Consider introduction of only those information sources that have relevance to the information needs of the students. Sometimes librarians feel they need to "teach" library skills by introducing every possible reference tool in the library. Introduce a few key tools, and then be prepared for the real teaching. The real teaching involves helping the student know when he or she has an information problem and helping the student think through the possibilities. This process begins to lead to many decisions that must be made concerning the quality of different information sources. Helping the student reason through to make such decisions is a strong beginning toward critical thinking.

3. Give time to brainstorming and the sharing of ideas. No student should do a research project in isolation. Group projects are best, so students can share ideas and responsibilities. Group projects are better when time is given for students to tell each other what they have found and what they

have not found. This allows students to begin to solve each others' information problems. Finally, every student project should have a final form in which it can be shared. Too much hard work and time are invested in a research project to simply hand it to the teacher. Broaden the audience. Have projects lead to displays, video programs, class presentations, or even a special magazine or newspaper that summarizes the students' work.

One of the most effective ways to end a unit in the library that demanded student selection of information is to post the results. On a large bulletin board, as a summary in the school's bulletin, or as an in-house library publication, the school librarian should show something like the following:

1. "Here are the 30 most interesting questions raised by Ms. Smith's class during the last semester, and here are the answers with the sources used." These 30 questions can be derived from the papers by the librarian, or better, by having each student identify the one most important question he or she answered.

2. (This second part is even more important.) "Here are 30 of the most important questions that Mrs. Smith's class found they *couldn't* answer. These questions will lead to the location of more information sources for next semester and, we hope, a series of new papers by the students next semester." This begins the process of students taking an initial broad topic and narrowing it to the hard and challenging questions that will demand new information sources for the library, and new research units. *(DC)*

BIBLIOGRAPHY

American Association of School Librarians and Association for Educational Communications and Technology. *Information Power: Guidelines for School Library Media Programs.* Chicago: American Library Association, 1988.
See pages 7–9. "...more emphasis on comprehension skills and less on decoding skills; less dependency on textbook programs and more individualized reading and research in all the content areas; and the use of literature as integral to, rather than as enrichment of, the language arts program."

Bertland, Linda H. "An Overview of Research in Metacognition: Implications for Information Skills Instruction." *School Library Media Quarterly* 14(2) (1986): 96–99.
A review of research which has direct relationship to planning the instruction of critical thinking skills. Teachers must serve as models and

critical thinkers themselves. Students must be encouraged to raise questions and to share and evaluate their questions.

Callison, Daniel. "School Library Media Programs and Free Inquiry Learning." *School Library Journal* 32(6) (1986): 20–24.
An outline of the elements of student-centered discovery and inquiry learning. School librarians have the opportunity to introduce such learning environments and must guard against reducing library skill education to nothing more than worksheets and location of meaningless facts.

Eisenberg, Michael. "Curriculum Mapping and Implementation of the Elementary School Library Media Skills Curriculum." *School Library Media Quarterly* 12(5) (1984): 411–18.
A systematic approach to gathering and evaluating information about the curriculum. Eisenberg has expanded his valuable methodology in cooperation with Robert E. Berkowitz. Their book *Resource Companion for Curriculum Initiative* (Ablex, 1988) provides ideas leading to identification of many units in a school's curriculum appropriate for integration with library media skills.

Haycock, Carol-Ann. "Information Skills in the Curriculum: Developing a School-Based Continuum." *Emergency Librarian* 13(1) (1985): 11–17.
Carol-Ann Haycock outlines a practical approach to teaching information skills. Three important areas presented here and often not included in other plans are analyzing information, recording information, and communicating or presenting information.

Kay, Linda H., and Jerry L. Young. "Socratic Teaching in Social Studies." *The Social Studies* 77(4) (1986): 158–61.
Teaching methods are reviewed in which students are taught to raise their own questions and to make predictions about possible answers. The process leads to a cycle in which the teacher may stimulate initial questions, but the student eventually begins to move through his or her own questioning cycle.

Krapp, JoAnn Vergona. "Teaching Research Skills: A Critical-Thinking Approach." *School Library Journal* 34(5) (1988): 32–35.
Some good ideas for getting started in this approach are given. Interaction through small groups is recommended as one element which helps students to identify and solve information problems.

Kuhlthau, Carol Collier. "Developing a Model of the Library Search Process: Cognitive and Affective Aspects." *RQ* 28(2) (1988): 232–42.
More than any other researcher today, Kuhlthau is refining and reshaping the way we should think about the typical secondary student's search for information and how that information is formulated into the typical term paper. Her work may very well lead to a new way of looking at how the term paper is assigned, evaluated, and how it should fit in the curriculum supported by library skill instruction units to meet specific student needs. School library media specialists in high schools around the country should give attention to her future publications in which she will describe additional insights to the student information search process based on a three-year research project underwritten by the Department of Education.

Rankin, Virginia. "One Route to Critical Thinking." *School Library Journal* 34(5) (1988): 27–31.
Discussion is given on actual projects in which students were encouraged to express their thoughts and experiences in a journal. The teacher and the librarian found many insights concerning the student's need for thinking through any library-related project. Student feedback was important in the evaluation of the library exercises.

School Library Media Quarterly 15(1) (1986).
This special issue is devoted to "Educating Students to Think." Excellent ideas are outlined to take students beyond simple library skills and on to programs which demand critical information choices by the student. The most important articles are: "Educating Students to Think: The Role of the School Library Media Program," by Jacqueline C. Mancall, Shirley L. Aaron, and Sue A. Walker; and "The Elementary School Library Media Teacher's Role in Educating Students to Think," by M. Ellen Jay.

School Library Media Quarterly 16(1) (1987).
This special issue of *SLMQ*, guest edited by Carol C. Kuhlthau, is devoted to "Information Skills: Tools for Learning." Articles which give several perceptions to the librarian's role in teaching critical thinking are provided. Leading authors include Betty P. Cleaver, Paula Montgomery, Jane Bandy Smith, Aldeen B. Markle, and Patricia Senn Breivik.

Sheingold, Karen. "Keeping Children's Knowledge Alive through Inquiry." *School Library Media Quarterly* 15(2) (1986): 80–85.
Karen Sheingold is Director of the Center for Children and Technology at the Bank Street College of Education. This article is the text of her 1986 speech to the American Library Association. She gives many examples of how to involve students in the inquiry method. This is very important reading for those who want to make the critical "question-answer-question cycle" meaningful to the student.

Smith, Adele. "The Library Media Specialist's Role in Promoting Critical Thinking Skills." In *School Library Media Annual 1986.* Edited by Shirley L. Aaron and Pat R. Scales, pp. 286–96. Littleton, CO: Libraries Unlimited, 1986.
A valuable guide to defining critical thinking skills based on Bloom's hierarchy of cognitive processes. Examples of critical thinking activities are given for an American history unit.

Stripling, Barbara K., and Judy M. Pitts. *Brainstorms & Blueprints: Teaching Library Research as a Thinking Process.* Englewood, CO: Libraries Unlimited, 1988.
Here is a clear and tested plan for developing research paper assignments based on critical thinking skills. An important concept presented by Stripling and Pitts is that students must be given time to think about the information sources they select. Students must reflect on each source as being usable and adequate. The student must ask:

    a. Have I found an acceptable variety of sources?
    b. Does the author of each source have acceptable qualifications?
    c. Do my sources represent a variety of points of view?
    d. Is the information biased?
    e. Is the information accurate and up-to-date?

Sullivan, Marjorie. "The Media Specialist and the Disciplined Curriculum." *The Journal of Education for Librarianship* 10(4) (1970): 286–95.

Sullivan ties the ideas of Jerome Bruner (*The Process of Education,* Cambridge: Harvard University Press, 1960) to the curriculum development role of the school library media specialist. This is one of several classic essays in our field which every professional school librarian should review for ideas and inspiration. Two others are: Frances Henne, "Learning to Learn in School Libraries," *School Libraries* 15 (4) (1966): 15–23; and Martin Rossoff, *The School Library and Educational Change,* Littleton, CO: Libraries Unlimited, 1971.

Case 9: The New Clerk

Description

After 14 years as the audiovisual clerk at JFK High School, Ruth Gleason is retiring. She has been, according to head media specialist Marcy Simmons, "a gift from Heaven." Ms. Gleason took on the audiovisual equipment and materials without hesitation. She learned to do minor maintenance and cleaning of equipment. She learned each machine's own "personal problems" and established a smooth scheduling process to allow the equipment to be used in the most efficient manner possible. Often, during the course of a day, one piece of equipment was moved by a student assistant among several classrooms in order to get the most use of the hardware. Ms. Gleason welcomed the microcomputer to the school as well. She even took some evening classes to become "computer literate" and kept all of the inventory and scheduling records on floppy disks.

Ms. Simmons has interviewed four potential replacements for Ms. Gleason with the understanding the principal wants a recommendation by next Monday. One of the four has worked as a parent volunteer for the past years. Her work has been related to Ms. Gleason's, as she has repaired many of the damaged filmstrips, made duplicate copies of videotape programs, and even learned to enter data for the automated book circulation system. "I know how to operate most of the equipment you have in the media center," she stated in the interview. "Because the student assistants have taught me so well, I even know which lamps go with what equipment." Ms. Simmon's recommendation to the principal has become obvious to her as the other three applicants have no experience in the media center operations.

When Ms. Simmons calls the principal on Monday morning, however, she is informed that during a Friday afternoon conference at the main administration building several decisions were made concerning hiring new personnel. The bottom line was that no new positions were to be created, and three were to be eliminated completely. The three displaced secretaries were to receive priority consideration for any clerical or secretarial openings in the district. Ms.

Simmons was informed that one of the secretaries was interested in the media center clerk position, even though it paid less than her present position. "At least I would have a job," she had said. The principal closes the conversation by making it clear the media clerk position will not be filled by anyone other than the displaced secretary, or the clerical position itself would be removed. Ms. Simmons is given a telephone number in order to contact the secretary and set a time to "get acquainted."

During the telephone conversation, Ms. Simmons is told by the secretary, "I type, I don't process or whatever it's called, and I don't intend to learn those floppy thingies. Equipment bothers me; I don't even have a dishwasher at home."

What can Ms. Simmons do to:

   a. Make the best of the situation if she has to accept this secretary in the media clerk's position?
   b. Attempt to show that the employment of the secretary as a part of the media center staff would be impossible?
   c. Explore all options before making a move to either accept or reject the new secretary?

ESTABLISH A JOB DESCRIPTION

Head media specialist Ms. Simmons needs to develop effective communication with her building principal. Ruth Gleason, the 14-year veteran audiovisual clerk, is considered "a gift from Heaven" and has willingly assumed responsibilities beyond those of a clerk, but her title of "clerk" would suggest that a displaced secretary should be able to assume the clerk's role without much difficulty. The media specialist needs to articulate Ms. Gleason's varied responsibilities to the principal (i.e., her initiative in caring for equipment, establishing a smooth scheduling process for the efficient use of the equipment, supervising student assistants and parent volunteers, and taking evening classes to become "computer-literate" and hence responsible for keeping inventory and scheduling records on floppy disk).

Furthermore, the media specialist ought to consider establishing a job description for the library media technician. In fact, desirable personal characteristics beyond job performance expectations are especially important for a library media technician to possess; such characteristics are an aptitude for library work, the ability to communicate clearly and to understand and follow written and oral directions, and a willingness to participate in formal and informal training on and off the job. *(SLR)*

DOCUMENT JOB PERFORMANCE

Given the situation, Ms. Simmons' options seem rather limited. With such a short time frame she will have to make decisions quickly. For now she will have to decide if she would rather work with an uncooperative clerk or have no help at all. If she decides to work with an uncooperative clerk, she must clearly define the clerk's duties and responsibilities. If there is no district job description for the library clerk, it would be extremely important to develop one as quickly as possible. It must be accurate, without tying the clerk into jobs or tasks that are too limited or being so all-encompassing that everyone in the building can utilize the clerk's time.

Once this has been done, Ms. Simmons must talk face to face with the new employee. All of the facts and job responsibilities must be clearly defined. Ms. Simmons needs to be extremely honest and open with the new clerk. She should explain that while she understands the secretary's feelings, the job requires that she perform certain tasks with which she may be unfamiliar. Ms. Simmons should explain that she will be documenting all activities and events. This will serve as a record, the means by which the new clerk's performance will be judged. With such documentation, standards of employment will be met or the employee will be replaced.

By accepting the clerk under these conditions Marcy allows the secretary to make a conscious and informed decision to adjust. It is possible that the clerk is intimidated, but given a chance, she may prove herself fully capable and cooperative. While the situation is unfortunate, Ms. Simmons owes it to the secretary and to the library program to attempt a workable compromise. *(VH)*

BIBLIOGRAPHY

American Association of School Librarians. Certification of School Media Specialists Committee. *Paraprofessional Support Staff for School Library Media Programs: A Competency Statement.* Chicago: American Library Association, 1978.
Gives specific job tasks for the library media aide and media technician.

American Association of School Librarians and Association for Educational Communications and Technology. *Information Power: Guidelines for School Library Media Programs.* Chicago: American Library Association, 1988.
See pages 62–65. "School and district personnel, as appropriate, develop job descriptions and evaluation procedures for support personnel."

Belker, Loren B. *The First-Time Manager.* New York: Amacom, 1978.
Chapter 8, "Hiring and Training of New Employees," gives some clear insight into the screening process, defines job expectations, and describes the training procedures for new employees.

Chernik, Barbara E. *Procedures for Library Media Technical Assistants.* Chicago: American Library Association, 1983.
This is an extensive guide to the tasks for media assistants. Support personnel jobs described include circulation procedures, supervision of audiovisual equipment, and processing of library materials. A sample job description is given.

Myers, Joan B. "Role of the Paraprofessional in the School Library." *American Libraries* 9(10) (1978): 602.
Myers argues for formal technical training in order to certify school library clerks as paraprofessionals.

Nitecki, Joseph Z. "Decision-Making and Library Staff Morale: Three Dimensions of a Two-Sided Issue." *Journal of Library Administration* 5 (1984): 59–78.
Reviews the relationship between staff morale and decision making in terms of variables in the operational, ethical, and work environment. Presents the disgruntled staff member, denied the job of his choice, as an example of an originator of job tension. Incorporates Maslow's hypothesis of needs hierarchy into the discussion of employee morale. Lists types of factors that influence job satisfaction and dissatisfaction. Defines the major components of the decision-making process.

Sever, Shmuel, and Fred Westcott. "Motivational Basis for Compensation Strategies in a Library Environment." *College & Research Libraries* 44 (1983): 228–35.
Reviews two dominant motivational theories in use. Suggests that the library environment motivates differently from an industrial or service work environment. Lists and explains the needs consistent with expectancy and reinforcement theories such as the need to belong, the need for power, the need for achievement, the need for competence, and the need for equity. Provides an annotated bibliography for further reading.

Case 10: Divided Programs

Description

Hawthorne District has an integrated media program, according to district media director. Jill Tyson, who joined the staff at Hawthorne City High School this fall as a media specialist, has reason to doubt this philosophy is valid. Frank Saxton, the other professional at Hawthorne High School, has always worked only with the audiovisuals. Mr. Saxton has taught 15 years. He started in the music department as orchestra director and became head of the fine arts department. Five years ago, after a mild heart attack, Mr. Saxton took an open audiovisual media position because he felt it would be less stressful and he had the required state AV certification as a minor on his master's degree.

Ms. Tyson worked in a junior high media center before her family's move to Hawthorne City. She loved using all kinds of resources, both print and nonprint; was looking forward to working with another professional; and expected to share all the tasks involved in running the integrated program of a large modern school library media center. Mr. Saxton does not want to share. He is only interested in the AV part of the program and is not very concerned about working with teachers. Demands for unexpected services make him nervous. He refuses to spend time helping students in the library. He is not comfortable with teaching instructional units to classes, even those that involve audiovisuals, and he has let Ms. Tyson know he will not be available for any of this work. He feels he should select all the nonprint materials and that Ms. Tyson should not do any AV curriculum work with teachers or students. Materials are kept separated in the two main rooms within the library facility. Mr. Saxton seldom enters the main library room, preferring to stay in the AV area, where he spends most of his time making signs for school events.

Ms. Tyson has spent 6 months trying friendly persuasion and is becoming desperate and depressed. She doesn't want to be just the book librarian. She needs help to make a change and decides to make an appointment with the district director, John Warren, to talk over her situation.

Consider the following:

a. Is there an argument for maintaining areas of specialization in a library media center?
b. How should Ms. Tyson approach Mr. Warren to make her argument for integration?
c. What are the problems a district director would have in getting Mr. Saxton involved?
d. Are there any approaches you could see available to Ms. Tyson? To the district director?

Response

GENERATE AN UNDERSTANDING OF RESPONSIBILITIES

Whenever two or more staff persons work in the same area there has to be a clear understanding of specific responsibilities for each assignment. This in no way precludes cooperation and sharing of duties. *(AR)*

EVALUATE THE PROGRAM

Ms. Tyson might approach Mr. Warren by suggesting they evaluate the present program, define areas that need improvement, and discuss ways to accomplish them to give her a better understanding of the effectiveness of the present program. She might suggest a committee be formed including the principal, representative staff members, students, and media personnel.

The evaluation tool could be internally designed or adapted from several already available (see Figure 7 for a sample media center philosophy).

The need for change is best documented to minimize conflict and resistance. Should a need for improvement be identified, then goals could be established and a plan of action outlined. *(AR)*

DIRECTOR MUST IMPLEMENT THE PLAN

Some hurdles of opposition could have already been cleared by the committee. Mr. Saxton is now aware of the changes that must be implemented to improve the program as charged by the committee and would feel some peer pressure from colleagues and administration to cooperate with the plan. His previous resistance might have been due to insecurity or lack of professional skills for tasks requested.

Figure 7. Media Center Philosophy

The Vigo County School Corporation recognizes that a media center is basic and essential to the educational program in every school.

As an integral part of every student's experience in school, the media center provides multiple and varied resources for all levels of the curriculum as well as for personal interests and recreational pursuits. It reinforces the school's goals to help students reach optimum intellectual, personal and social maturity, enabling them to become productive, contributing individuals. Specifically, it seeks to develop self-directed learning, as well as reading for pleasure and personal information with concurrent establishment of lifetime learning skills; to foster critical reading, listening, and viewing experiences upon which to formulate sound decision-making skills; to teach research skills that enable the child to locate and utilize the resources available; and to encourage the implementation of a wide variety of resources to extend and enhance the quantity and quality of informational material available.

The media center serves as a laboratory for students to apply and extend their basic skills in all areas of learning. It, in fact, becomes the individualized learning center for all levels of academic growth.

In order to achieve this concept, provisions need to be made to provide a qualified professional director, a physical facility adequate to house the necessary equipment and materials, a program developed to circulate and disseminate information and materials available, and maximum accessibility within confines of the school day to accommodate optimum student/staff utilization. The media center director brings a wealth of expertise to the staff and can be a valuable asset to the educational program of the school. This person coordinates the selection of materials, plans and implements the goals of the center, provides expertise on curriculum and textbook committees, serves as a resource member on instructional committees, and promotes optimum usage of school and community resources that will bring together an environment that assures the most positive and successful learning experience for each and every user.

Reprinted with permission from the Vigo County School Corporation, 961 Lafayette Avenue, P.O. Box 4331, Terre Haute, IN 47804-2994.

The district director is challenged with providing the vehicle to achieve quality service. This is the primary goal. The assigning and utilizing of staff must complement this goal. Involving the administration and professional staff fosters positive support and strengthens internal implementation. If all aspects of the situation are handled in a professional manner with the primary common goal of quality service for maximum performance, professional staff will respond to the challenge and perform to achieve the goal. Performance is significantly correlated to purpose and expectations (see Figure 8 for a sample school media specialist job description).

Mr. Warren should capitalize on the talents and skills of each employee and integrate those talents into a carefully planned program to achieve desired results.

Insecurity is a common factor when one is asked to perform without basic knowledge of a task. Reaction to insecurity takes many forms. Resistance is one such form. It does not necessarily reflect inability if proper direction and guidance are provided. *(AR)*

Figure 8. Job Description—School Media Specialist

The media specialist, educated in teaching techniques, librarianship, and media brings to the job knowledge of teacher and pupil needs in relation to the curriculum. His/Her knowledge of instructional materials is necessary for building and maintaining a materials collection and for working with teachers and pupils in the areas of curriculum and personal needs. The responsibilities of the media specialist have expanded greatly due to public awareness, the current growth of informational technology, and new programs implemented by the Vigo County School Corporation such as:

1. Primetime classes
2. Academically talented classes
3. Computer literacy and computer assisted instruction
4. Developmental kindergarten
5. Future problem solving programs
6. The expansion of special education classes
7. Creative writing programs
8. Media fairs
9. Assertive discipline programs
10. Preventive substance abuse programs
11. "On-the-job" career training programs
12. Law related educational programs
13. State mandated increased graduation requirements
14. Statewide competency testing programs

Professional duties inherent to the role of the media specialist are:

1. Guiding pupils in thinking, listening, viewing, and reading
2. Assisting teachers in developing informational reference and research skills of students.
3. Providing in-service training for teachers and students in the preparation and utilization of instructional materials.
4. Evaluating, previewing, and selecting materials from professional sources for purchase for the school.
5. Identifying materials for reinforcing the curriculum.
6. Communicating with the staff the availability of materials.
7. Teaching the use of informational and technological skills.
8. Developing and maintaining a well organized facility.
9. Continuing to evaluate, alter, update, and expand the media program including print materials, software, and hardware.
10. Supplying teachers with materials in all areas of the curriculum.
11. Serving on curricular planning programs, textbook adoption committees and other committees both at a building and system-wide level.
12. Maintaining basic equipment to fulfill the demands of the program.

Reprinted with permission from the Vigo County School Corporation, 961 Lafayette Avenue, P.O. Box 4331, Terre Haute, IN 47804-2994.

INTERCHANGEABLE PARTS

To separate competencies of the professional school library media specialist into the two categories of "audiovisual director," and "librarian" places the profession in the "Stone Age" of its evolution. Although it may be wise for one professional to specialize in nonprint materials and another to specialize in reference services and young adult literature, all certified library media center professionals should be able to cover any territory from microcomputers to encyclopedias. The given management situation demonstrates how the failure on one person's part to fully expand his knowledge base and to be competent in a vast array of school library media services clearly prevents both of the professionals from performing at the highest levels possible.

To put it bluntly, such fossils as Frank Saxton should be removed from the ranks of the media professionals and should either leave the school system or be placed in clerical roles. Mr. Saxton is an example of an individual who has been moved from one place to another until his seniority has allowed for him to be placed in a position of command over one who is younger but has a proven record of success. The "AV person" and the "librarian" must both be placed in the position of professionals who teach students, consult with teachers, and strive to advance the services of the media center. It may be that Frank could be motivated to move in a more professional direction through in-service training and a new job description. I have not seen many of the "rocks" change, however. *(DC)*

BIBLIOGRAPHY

American Association of School Librarians and Association for Educational Communications and Technology. *Information Power: Guidelines for School Library Media Programs.* Chicago: American Library Association, 1988.
See pages 56–68. "The success of any school library media program, no matter how well designed, depends ultimately on the quality and number of the personnel responsible for the program."

Gillespie, John T., and Diana L. Spirt. *Administering the School Library Media Center.* New York: R.R. Bowker Company, 1983.
Chapter 2 deals with the "Functions of the School Library Media Center," and chapter 5 provides detailed job descriptions for "Staff." Professionals are described as teachers, planners, consultants, and evaluators. Job descriptions which include scheduling equipment, operating equipment, maintaining inventory, and other such tasks are identified as either paraprofessional or nonprofessional.

Loertscher, David. "School Library Media Centers: The Revolutionary Past" and "The Second Revolution: A Taxonomy for the 1980s." *Wilson Library Bulletin* 56(6) (1982): 415–21.
Describes how the "traditional roles of audiovisual technician and librarian have merged to form the professional role of instructional developer."

Prostano, Emanuel T., and Joyce S. Prostano. *The School Library Media Center.* Littleton, CO: Libraries Unlimited, 1987.
The media technician is described as one who reports to the school library media specialist. Technicians specialize in production of audiovisual programs, operation of equipment, and maintenance of equipment. The media specialist manages the program and holds a vast array of competencies from teaching to budgeting, from analysis of data to evaluation of instruction, from selection of materials to long-range planning and policy development.

Case 11: Equality for All: Is It Practical?

Description

Lois Oakley is pleased with the progress she has made in developing the library media program in Lincoln Middle School. In just 2 years, she has integrated the collection with the curriculum, worked on instructional units with almost half of the teachers, and involved most of the students in some activity related to media center use.

Rita McKenzie has 12 mildly mentally retarded students in her special education class. Ms. McKenzie has been vocal in her praise of Ms. Oakley and her policies. Ms. McKenzie's students enjoy being treated like all other students. This librarian teams with Ms. McKenzie to teach these special kids library skills, and Ms. Oakley has given several book talks in Ms. McKenzie's class to encourage reading and learning through the library. No child is made to feel slow or worthless.

Today, at the annual teacher orientation, Ms. McKenzie asked Ms. Oakley if some of her students could serve as library helpers during the coming school year. She told Ms. Oakley how good they would feel to be useful to the school and how much they like her.

Ms. Oakley, whose criteria for student volunteers include maintaining at least a B grade average, being able to pass a media skills test, and taking responsibility to work at times with little supervision, is appalled at the thought of using even the best of these special education students as volunteers. She knows the individual effort and time it would take to make them useful as helpers. Time spent here would reduce some of her service elsewhere. Her goal to involve even more of the teachers in her program would suffer. Her plan to incorporate additional reading programs this year would be delayed.

Consider the following:

a. Is there a place for students from special education classes as volunteers in the school library media program?

b. In what ways might the training of special education students differ from the regular student volunteer program?

   c. If Ms. Oakley says no to these students and does not include
them as helpers, what does it do to her credibility as someone
who cares for all students?

Response

IS THERE A PHILOSOPHY OF SERVICE?

The stated purpose of most library/media centers is to serve the
school community of which they are a part. That community includes
the administration, teachers, and students—all students.

The ordinary function of a special education instructor is to
prepare students for an active and productive adult life. Frequently,
such preparation includes concrete learning experiences that can be
carried over. What better combination can education have than a
department whose function is to serve paired with a department
whose function is to find service outlets for students? It seems to
represent, at least at first glance, a symbiotic educational relationship.

There is a place for every student in the media center. Unlike the
old-fashioned "library," the media center concept is one of change
and flexibility—meeting the demands of a rapidly changing technology. Media specialists must be able to be flexible in a profession
whose duties continue to grow and the number of hours in which to
do them is reduced. Jobs must be delegated, and perfectionism will
be sacrificed in order to cover all the bases. With some forethought
and planning, Ms. McKenzie's mentally retarded students can function successfully as student assistants. *(DP)*

SELECT TRAINEES CAREFULLY

Even with these good feelings and cooperation from all parties
involved, special preparations would need to be made, including
appropriate screening to establish selection criteria and a defined
training program for those accepted. Part of the training might be a
contract which would state that either party could withdraw during
the training, without, it is hoped, encountering hard feelings.

EXAMPLE SELECTION STANDARDS:

   1. Dependable attendance—Low absence rate
   2. Academic accomplishment—The special education teacher
      must feel that time given to the media center would not
      jeopardize the student's classroom standing
   3. Self-initiative—Desire to listen, to take direction, and to fol-
      low routine

4. Communication skills—Willingness to deal with fellow students, not just personal classmates *(VH)*

CHOOSE TASKS THAT WILL LEAD TO SUCCESS

My feeling is that once one of these mildly mentally retarded students learns a procedure, he or she could perform it daily with success. The important point is to initially choose repetitive tasks that are easily learned, such as picking up the mail, dusting, watering plants, straightening chairs, returning periodicals to the shelves, taking overdue notices to teachers' boxes, arranging the encyclopedias numerically or alphabetically, helping move equipment, and stamping selected items with the school name. *(VLW)*

PLAN TOGETHER THE NEEDED TRAINING

The two teachers should plan together for the integration of library-related skills instruction in the classroom before bringing special students into the media center. The basics of alphabetization and number order should be stressed. The four basic mathematics functions should be mastered. Later, the concepts of filing and shelving can be introduced.

If such instruction takes place in the classroom, Ms. Oakley can become involved with the students and gain their confidence. She will learn which library jobs are suitable for each student. As the special education student gains confidence, library jobs can be taken to the classroom for completion. Filing, alphabetizing, and sorting lend themselves well to this situation. Later, the special education students can be brought to the media center to function on a day-by-day basis, returning as needed to the classroom. While in the media center, the special education students can begin the same training as other media assistants. At times, Ms. McKenzie's students could be paired with non-special education student assistants, resulting in a mutual learning situation. *(DP)*

INDIVIDUALIZE THE TRAINING

With such a program, it is essential that tasks be assigned that can be handled by the student. Each student's skills and abilities, as well as disabilities, would need to be identified and accounted for. Training for special students would also have to be done on an individual basis. Each student should be shown the basics and then trained on more specific tasks that he or she could handle. While these students might not work best under pressure, it is important they be given some regular jobs to perform. Special students should be encouraged, under close supervision, to check books out for students and faculty. *(VH)*

WORK TOWARD A COMPROMISE

It seems, in this situation, necessary to reach a compromise. I suppose that the federal, state, and local moneys divested in the special education programs cause people to give weighted attention to the observations expressed by special education teachers. Even when they say they don't want their students treated differently, they do expect exceptions to be made and can apply subtle or more direct pressures when they feel it necessary. In this case, compromise is possible if Lois Oakley can accept fully the premise that there is a place for special education students as library volunteers. Usually in any school these students love the library if given gentle and friendly direction.

What the media specialist needs to do is get rid of her elitist attitude. Failure to do so will destroy her credibility as one who cares for *all* students.

Extra training could be the responsibility of the special education teacher (with very little extra help from the librarian). The special education teacher would likely welcome the opportunity to involve the students in learning practical skills. Other student volunteers could also help supervise under a buddy system. The librarian needs to be able to delegate more responsibility to others. She does not have to give extra individual time to these students.

There are a number of examples where special education students have been very successful volunteers. In the fall of 1979 at Coventry Elementary School at Crystal Lake, Illinois, learning disabled students from grades 4 to 6 were used to tutor second graders in library skills. It was found that learning disabled students who are trained in library media skills can be effective tutors of younger non-learning disabled students in performing the same skills.

In the Monroe County Public Library (Bloomington, Indiana), autistic students as well as students who are severely retarded help in the library two times a week. They are able to put away paperbacks, stamp books, shelve books, and do other similar clerical chores. This work is supervised by an aide and so it involves little effort from the librarians who need only see that there is work left for these students to do. The key is making sure that the teacher will do the training and this person or an aide will supervise the work. *(KM)*

BIBLIOGRAPHY

Baker, Philip D. *The Library Media Program and the School.* Littleton, CO: Libraries Unlimited, 1984.
This book presents recommendations on many matters related to the organization, administration, and supervision of school library media programs. A chapter covers services and programs that the school library media program offers to special user constituencies, such as the bilingual learner, the student of English as a second language (ESL), the gifted and talented learner, the emotionally disturbed, and the physically and mentally limited users.

Baskin, Barbara Holland, and Karen H. Harris, eds. *The Special Child in the Library.* Chicago: American Library Association, 1976.
This handbook presents a philosophical base for procedures, information on materials, examples of creative programs, and guidelines for modification of facilities. Not really out of date, these readings offer much for the librarian to consider in making the school library an open place for the special student.

Roberts, Beverly J., and Isabel Schon. "Student Aides in Arizona School Libraries: A Descriptive Study." *School Library Journal* 31(9) (1985): 32–35.
This survey reported many of the positive aspects of using student aides: (1) growth experiences for the students; (2) good community public relations; (3) allows for wider range of library services; (4) frees the professional media specialist from mundane jobs. Lists tasks assigned to student aides although few given are "academic." Nearly half of the librarians surveyed indicated that "handicapped students are welcome to serve as student aides."

Zettel, Jeffery J., and Alan Abeson. "Litigation, Law, and the Handicapped." *School Library Media Quarterly* 6(4) (1978): 234–45.
A study of the judicial and legislative accomplishments of the handicapped, culminating with the passage of Public Law 94–142. *SLMQ* ran a special issue on P.L. 94–142 the following year [8(1) (1979)].

Case 12: Leaving the Teaching to the Librarian

Description

For the past 3 years the school librarian, Sara Lukes, has provided extensive bibliographic instruction for each freshman English class. The instruction has included orientation to the basic use of the card catalog and the periodical indexes as well as a few basic reference tools. The instruction usually takes three class periods. The instruction has been planned and developed with the English department and each of the four English teachers usually follows the instruction with assignments that require the student to use the skills learned in the library.

This year a new English teacher, Patti McCall, has joined the faculty. This is the first year of teaching for Ms. McCall. In addition, two units of freshman English have been added to Jim Wilson's teaching schedule. He has taught geography classes at the school before, but the number of geography classes has been reduced to three and Mr. Wilson now faces these two new English classes for the first time. Mr. Wilson's other responsibilities include coaching the basketball team. He has been with the school for 14 years.

When it comes time for the annual bibliographic instructional unit both Ms. McCall and Mr. Wilson agree to send their classes to the library, but neither remains with the class as the other English teachers do. Ms. McCall indicates that she does not plan to assign her students any activities that will reinforce the library skills. Mr. Wilson also indicates that such instruction is a "nice break" for him, but he does not see any reason for assigning a paper which will take a great deal of time to grade. Besides, both of them argue, they were never required to use the library when they were in junior high school. "Such skills should be taught in high school."

As Ms. Lukes, the media specialist, consider the following:

   a. Why is it important for teachers to attend library instruction with their class?

b. What can be done to involve Ms. McCall and Mr. Wilson in the "enforcement" of the bibliographic instruction?
c. Is it always necessary that the librarian give orientation and bibliographic instruction, or can teachers assume some of the instructional role as well?
d. In what ways should teachers and librarians share the teaching role in the proper use of library materials?

Response

EVALUATE, INTEGRATE, AND TEAM-TEACH

The first reason teachers should attend library instruction is skill reinforcement. If teachers view bibliographic instruction as "useless" or a "nice break," that attitude will prevail among the students. Teachers should realize (or be made to realize) they are setting an example for student attitude toward the library.

Second, since the students are freshmen, the librarian has had limited contact with them. For discipline and control purposes, the teacher's presence is important. Certainly, in my case I have found this to be true. In my school, with this fall's library instruction up to ten sections of freshmen, I had five of the six teachers actively attending and participating. In the class of the one teacher who was not there, problems arose, eventually ending in the students fighting in the library. This was the first time in 10 years there had been any difficulty, and I lay the problem at the feet of the absent teacher.

Some possible action would be to enlist the aid of cooperative teachers or departments. Show Ms. McCall and Mr. Wilson there is a need for bibliographic instruction at some point in the student's school career. Emphasis should be placed on its value to individual students over the long run. The librarian might also volunteer to show teachers how easily reinforcement of library skills could be worked into their plans. Many teachers think library skills will add to their already overwhelming work load. Some personalized public relations could work wonders.

Another plan is to do the grading for the bibliographic unit and give the scores to the teachers. During my 3-day orientation I give daily assignments and grade them each night. Each teacher has the option to include these grades as part of the semester grade or as extra-credit points. Most teachers appreciate a 3-day break from direct teaching, while also getting daily grades to measure performance.

Ideally, bibliographic skills should be taught as a team effort. The librarian is the logical choice to give initial library orientation, but a teacher's input can reinforce what is being presented. Our orientation is done through the social studies department because English is "too busy with important things." As materials are presented, the teachers will point out other uses or emphasize the importance of that item in the future. This is great for two reasons: It shows the students that teachers do use the library, and it shows them that this unit isn't an isolated part of learning. If students know they will need to use information and resources later, they tend to pay closer attention to the initial instruction. The teacher can also serve an instructional role by being aware of individual student differences. In 3 days I can't begin to touch on more than the basics. If the teacher knows what was presented, he or she can build on that knowledge.

Through such combined efforts we can help destroy one of our worst enemies, the image of the librarian as the "protector of the books." Active involvement in planning, teaching, and evaluation will help us improve our image and status as librarians, and serve to educate teachers about our role in education. *(VH)*

SET POLICY

This case involves not only role designation and comprehension by all parties concerned, but a definite need for public/human relations in working with these two teachers. If there is support from the school administration, several options are available, among which are the following:

1. Direct response from the principal about what is expected of the teachers
2. The opportunity for the librarian to give a demonstration of strategies and implementation of a joint project during a faculty meeting
3. Preparation and distribution of a policy/procedures handbook for effectively working with classes to enhance instruction (Note: Make sure the handbook has a preface stating the librarian's philosophy and role in the instructional program.)

If there is no administrative support, however, the problem is magnified. It should not be forgotten that the children are the ones who suffer. Much more has to be done to win the confidence and understanding of the two teachers. Perhaps the new English teacher can be persuaded by one who has been there considerably longer and takes an active role in the library program. *(DZP)*

BIBLIOGRAPHY

American Association of School Librarians and Association for Educational Communications and Technology. *Information Power: Guidelines for School Library Media Programs.* Chicago: American Library Association, 1988.
See pages 20–24. "Classroom teachers and library media specialists work together in developing skills for learning throughout life, including appreciation and enjoyment of all types of communication media."

Turner, Philip M. "Research on Helping Teachers Teach." *School Library Media Quarterly* 15(4) (1987): 229–31.
Turner summarizes much of his important work in attempting to identify those major factors which lead to the media specialist making a positive contribution to the teaching environment, especially in the role as team teacher. His books, *Helping Teachers Teach* and *Casebook for Helping Teachers Teach* are extremely useful.

Case 13: Written Policies and Consistent Action

Description

Sara Davies was in her second year as a school media specialist at Washington Junior High School. She had continued the policy of charging fines for materials returned late. This provided some "petty cash" in order to purchase materials and supplies without going through the paperwork of requesting such items through her regular media center budget.

Sharon Fast, a student who seemed to want to check out all of the books from the library, and who never returned materials on time, was in the process of paying her latest fine. As Sharon gave Ms. Davies a five-dollar bill and waited for change, John Bailey slipped into the librarian's office with a book in his hand. "Here it is, Ms. Davies," said John. "I know I'm late in returning it, but this is my first time." "No problem," replied Ms. Davies. "I won't charge you because I know you will do better in the future."

Ms. Davies was also experiencing constant problems with teachers scheduling classes on short notice, not returning materials borrowed for private or classroom use, and asking for materials to be ordered after the deadline for requests. In some cases she was able to work out an agreement with the teacher, but in other cases emotions had flared on either her part or the teacher's. Of course, no fines were charged to teachers for late return of materials.

Ms. Davies was also often worried about challenges that might be made by local parents concerning some of the books recommended in the school media center selection guides. It seemed there should be a way to manage these issues, but she never had the time to address them. The best approach, she thought, was simply not to purchase any materials that might cause objections.

There was nothing in writing which explained the operation or philosophy of the media program. Teachers, students, parents, and the principal often asked her questions about operations and usually were satisfied with her answers, even though she might give a different response to the same question.

As Ms. Davies, consider the following:

a. What is the obligation of the school media specialist to establish and implement written policy and procedures?
b. What benefits come from developing written policies?
c. Discuss methods which might be useful to Ms. Davies in planning and implementing such written policies.

Response

ESTABLISH DIRECTION AND CONTINUITY

Ms. Davies is representative of many school media specialists who, because of lack of time, lack of knowledge or lack of expertise in policymaking, lack of understanding of the benefits of policies, lack of administrative support, and/or other factors, fail to develop written policies and procedures. In Ms. Davies' situation, the absence of policies caused inconsistent decisions, which result in confusion and probable feelings of unfairness among patrons, in a lack of clarity about the program, and in haphazard collection development and management practices.

Ms. Davies could benefit greatly from having policies and procedures for operating the media center. Well thought-out written policies based on the philosophy, goals, and objectives of both the district and media programs give direction and continuity to a program. Policies provide a record of past decisions and a guide for future actions. When decisions are based on written policy, they are more consistent. Media center management becomes more efficient because less time is spent reconsidering similar problems. Printed policies improve communication by letting the faculty, students, parents, and administrators know the basis on which the program is conducted, thereby contributing to a sense of organization, dependability, and efficiency. Furthermore, patrons feel assured knowing that everyone is treated in the same manner, and relations with the media staff are much improved.

Who is responsible for setting policy? The elected governing body of the school district is legally responsible for policymaking. However, the superintendent is generally given the task of recommending and drafting proposed policies. The superintendent may, in turn, delegate the work of developing specific policies to persons with specialized knowledge. For policies relating to the library media program, the superintendent may well request that the district library media director or other school media professional prepare the policy statements.

Rebecca Bingham states that one of the primary responsibilities of a district media director is "planning and developing policies." Numerous publications state that the media specialist should be involved in developing media policies, but little has been written on exactly how to carry out that charge. *(HRA)*

INVOLVING OTHERS CAN CREATE ALLIANCE

Approaches to policy development vary according to such factors as the size of the district, board practice, administrative structure, current policies or the lack thereof, and local tradition. There is no one best way to proceed. However, if the media specialist accepts this responsibility, policy development should not be undertaken in a vacuum. Better policies will be created if representatives from the student body, faculty, administration, and community are involved in the process. Indeed, the more who participate and invest their ideas, the stronger the final document. By involving a range of individuals in policy development and having the board of education adopt the policies, Ms. Davies would be building valuable alliances within the "school community" while strengthening her program.

As one approach to policy development, Ms. Davies might want to consider the process used successfully by the Rosholt School District's media program. It involves 10 steps: (1) laying the groundwork, (2) selecting policies, (3) reviewing the literature and writing initial drafts, (4) obtaining external advice, (5) working with policy advisory committees, (6) seeking administrative input, (7) finalizing drafts, (8) adopting policies, (9) implementing the policies, and (10) revising the policies. For more details on the process, consult *School Media Policy Development: A Practical Process for Small Districts.* While the process was originally developed for a district serving under 1,000 students, it could apply equally well to larger districts. *(HRA)*

PLACE POLICY IN PRINT, BUT BE READY TO REVISE

Following adoption by the board of education, the policies should be implemented immediately and be made readily available in school offices and the media centers. To further clarify and promote the program, a media program handbook could be assembled that includes not only the board-approved library media policies but also building-level procedures and guidelines, job descriptions, a listing of program services, a program philosophy and long-range plans for the program, personnel data, access information including circulation rules for students and staff and hours of operation, the library media skills curriculum, and the budget. Since a handbook of this type could readily help answer questions about the media program's operation, it could be very useful to Ms. Davies.

In conclusion, there are two important points to emphasize. While creating policies is the goal, the development process itself often produces an additional unexpected benefit. Those who are involved in policy development enlarge their personal knowledge of the program and often become enthusiastic supporters and highly motivated "lobbyists" for program improvement. Furthermore, it is also important to stress that simply developing policies is not the sole answer. Policies must be implemented correctly, carried out in a consistent manner, and reviewed on a regular basis for possible revision. Policy development is an ongoing process which must be continued if it is to be effective. *(HRA)*

BIBLIOGRAPHY

Adams, Helen R. *School Media Policy Development: A Practical Process for Small Districts.* Littleton, CO: Libraries Unlimited, 1986.
An excellent guide for the development of policies in many areas of school library program management. Adams bases her procedures on experiences and the literature. She shows the value of involving parents, teachers, and administrators and always being ready to revise policies to establish fair and workable guidelines.

American Association of School Librarians and Association for Educational Communications and Technology. *Information Power: Guidelines for School Library Media Programs.* Chicago: American Library Association, 1988.
See pages 29–31, 48–55. "Library media professionals at all levels must become knowledgeable about policy areas that restrict or limit the quality and quantity of activities and services for students and teachers."

Gordon, Lee Diane. "Put It in Writing: The Policy and Procedure Manual." *The Book Report* 4(3) (1985): 17–19.
A concise outline of the various issues a policy and procedure manual should address.

Kemp, Betty, ed. *School Library and Media Center Acquisitions Policies and Procedures.* 2nd ed. Phoenix, AZ: Oryx Press, 1986.
A compilation of sample policies, this is a very useful guide. Also of great use is the first edition edited by Mary M. Taylor. Together, these two books will provide most of the constructive leads to help a school librarian draft a collection development policy.

Meyers, Judith. "Policy and Policymaking for School Library Media Specialists." In Vol. 1 of *School Library Media Annual 1983.* Edited by Shirley L. Aaron and Pat R. Scales, pp. 185–96. Littleton, CO: Libraries Unlimited, 1983..
This is a clear definition of what policy *is* and is *not*. Meyers gives valuable guidance in answering such questions as, "How are policies implemented?" and "Why are policies important?"

Case 14: Bible Study in the Library

Description

Greentown is a small Midwestern town. The population has a high percentage of "fundamentalists" and the largest church in town has often actively supported prayer in the schools and Bible study for young adults in any environment, including the church, the home, business, and schools.

Several high school students carry Bibles to school and are often seen reading privately in study hall, at lunch, and at other free moments during the school day. Velma Mager, school library media specialist, has also observed that many students come to the library early in the morning to wait for school to begin and will gather in small groups either to read the Bible or to quietly conduct daily devotions. She has never stopped such activity as long as it did not prevent others from using the library before school. Ms. Mager is a member of the local Methodist church, and she has never observed any students from her church taking part in the devotional activities.

Diane Allison, the principal of the small high school, informs Ms. Mager that, beginning next Monday morning, the two small meeting rooms in the library will be used for formal study by any student who wants to take part in "Bible Study and Devotions." The sessions will be "supervised" by Ed Johnston, the school's biology teacher who is also a member of a local fundamentalist church. Students may attend on a voluntary basis, but the two rooms will be off limits before school for any other uses. One room houses the nonprint collection and is often used as a preview room. The other is used for small-group discussion and meetings and houses the special career materials collection.

As Ms. Mager, consider:

    a. How would you respond to such demands from the principal?
    b. What responsibility does the school library have to any student activity that includes reading and discussing religious concepts, beliefs, and other literature?

c. In what manner does the principle of separation of church and state apply in this situation?

Response

ASSIGN ANOTHER AREA

The principal should be informed that the areas she assigned to the religious study groups were used by other teachers and students for school-educational purposes at the times the study groups were assigned to them. Therefore, another area should be assigned to the religious groups. If the school is open as a meeting place for community groups during nonschool hours, should it not be open to this group as well? This might be especially true since the group is representative of such a large segment of the local community.

The library's responsibility to the religious study groups would be to provide materials representing as many different viewpoints on controversial subjects as possible—a reflection of a well-balanced selection policy. *(MMJ)*

AN INFORMAL MEETING, NOT COMPULSORY

On the surface, the problem posed here does not appear difficult. Assuming that the principal involved is a manager and not a dictator of school affairs, the librarian should discuss the situation with her. The principal should be made aware that the meeting rooms in the library serve various functions and are often in use before school by both staff and students. Making the rooms off limits during that time, to all but those in the study group, would deny the needs of other patrons. The media specialist should point out that, for some time, the library has allowed, and will continue to allow, these students to gather informally.

The library's responsibility for such an activity is no different from its responsibility to any group wishing to read about and discuss a topic. A legal case could be made if students were required to attend the sessions, but informal meetings to discuss religious ideas are not illegal. As long as the meetings are not sanctioned by the school and attendance is not compulsory, the separation of church and state exists. *(JP)*

BIBLIOGRAPHY

Ares, Charles E. "Religious Meetings in the Public High School: Freedom of Speech or Establishment of Religion?" *University of California, Davis, Law Review* 20(2) (1987): 313–38.
An extensive review of opinions given in various court cases concerning the definition of "establishment of religion" in the public schools.

Boardman, Edna M. "Looking for a Better Religious Balance in Your Curriculum? Try the Library." *American School Board Journal* 175(1) (1988): 37.
An interesting statement in which the librarian describes how students and teachers may have free and open access to information beyond the textbook through the school library. The limitations of coverage by instructional materials concerning the many aspects of religion are met by the development of a solid reference collection as well as a variety of biographies and novels. Such an approach to balance the curriculum is true not only for the study of "religious heritage" but for most other areas of the curriculum as well.

McCarthy, Martha M. "Religion and Public Schools: Emerging Legal Standards and Unresolved Issues." *Harvard Educational Review* 55(3) (1985): 278–317.
This in-depth look at issues relating to religion and the public schools is valuable reading for all school personnel. McCarthy is an established expert in this area, and her coverage of the issues is clear and complete. The author's work illuminates the sensitive issues involved and the current Supreme Court's stand in applying First Amendment guarantees in public schools.

Peach, Lucinda. "Supreme Court Docket: Does Religion Belong in the Schools?" *Social Education* 50(3) (1986): 166–69.
Reviews First Amendment case law and briefly presents the 1985 Supreme Court case findings for *Bender vs. Williamsport Area School District,* which dealt with whether a Bible study group could use school property during an organized, school-sponsored activity period.

"Religious Training, Free Speech: What New Supreme Court Decisions Mean." *U.S. News and World Report* May 9, 1952: 27.
In 1952, the U.S. Supreme Court ruled that public school districts could conduct release-time religious education programs, but only if classes are held no more than one hour per week and not on school grounds. Reactions to this ruling are found in the following sources: "The Court Concurs," *The Christian Century* May 14, 1952, 582–83; Greenbaum, Edward S. "The Parent's Right to Choose," *The Nation* February 9, 1952, 128–130; Thayer, V.T., "A Crutch for Churches," *The Nation* February 9, 1952, 130–32.

Case 15: New Kid on the Block

Description

Hal Mead had just been hired as the new assistant school media specialist at Cranfield North High School. Cranfield is one of two large high schools, each with a student enrollment of 2,800. The media staff at each high school is composed of two full-time librarians and two full-time clerks. Mr. Mead is fresh from library school but taught for four years at a high school very similar to CNHS. He was a successful teacher and became interested in a career as a school librarian after 3 years of using the school library extensively with his social studies students. Mr. Mead is certified to teach history, speech and drama, and English. He sees the school media center as a great opportunity to work with teachers and develop a strong independent study program.

Mr. Mead was hired by the Cranfield Public School District to head a junior high school library for a few years and gain some experience in the library area before moving to a senior high school job. He took the position but was notified just 10 days before school started in the fall that the assistant position would be open at the high school. He was offered the post and agreed to take it without talking with the head librarian, who has been in that position for the past 8 years.

Robert Snyder has been fairly successful as the head librarian at Cranfield North. Before he came, few teachers attempted to use the media center and there was very little money spent on nonprint materials and equipment. "Mr. Snyder brought us into the twentieth century," several teachers would proclaim. For about a dozen of the 133 teachers, he was a "master teacher." With these teachers Mr. Snyder worked very closely and teamed on several instructional units through the use of the library. Mr. Snyder's former assistant, who moved with her husband to Denver 2 weeks prior to the start of the school year, had no interest in working with teachers. She would field reference questions but was more comfortable in managing the circulation desk and ordering books.

Although Mr. Snyder had no prior classroom teaching experience, he felt very positive about his team-teaching efforts.

Two days before school opens, Mr. Snyder and Mr. Mead meet for the first time. By the end of that first day, Mr. Snyder has made it clear to Mr. Mead that as the head media specialist he will make all contacts with teachers on instructional matters. As the head media specialist, he will give all bibliographic instruction units, evaluate students, and determine materials that will be used to support instructional units either from the current collection or to be placed on order. Mr. Mead is to manage the circulation system with a goal of setting up an automated system over the next 2 years. Mr. Mead should also weed the vertical file before the end of his first year as assistant librarian. However, Mr. Mead is not to approach teachers or plan units with teachers.

As Mr. Mead, how would you:

a. Attempt to prove that you can do more?
b. Make sure you knew more about the job before you agreed to take the position?
c. Plan to develop any professional relationship with the teaching staff?

Response

BE SURE OF THE JOB EXPECTATIONS

Mr. Mead made a big mistake by not talking to this head librarian before taking the position. It is always advisable to look at the library facility and at least speak with the people who will be working with you on a new job. If a co-worker's philosophy is diametrically opposed to yours, life will be difficult. An understanding should be reached before signing a contract. If possible, Mr. Mead should have considered other schools.

Mr. Mead might try to "make the best of it." He has to convince Mr. Snyder that he can work with teachers and that he is not a threat because of his past successful teaching experience. He must show Mr. Snyder that the best curriculum involvement program needs two "master" teachers and will provide more options for the faculty.

He might try flattery. After a few months, he might mention how much he admires the head librarian and ask for help in becoming as good at involving teachers as the head librarian seems to be. "I might be transferred to another school some day, and I'll need to know how to do this," Mr. Mead might note. *(JM)*

MAKE THE MOVE OR MOVE OUT

Mr. Mead has 121 of 133 teachers who need support and are not getting it from Mr. Snyder. This group is bound to have two or three people who can be cultivated as "planning partners" with Mr. Mead. If those teachers ask for help, Mr. Mead should proceed to provide it, regardless of Mr. Snyder's reaction. Once Mr. Mead has been successful with one or two teachers, the word will get out and the demand will grow. If Mr. Snyder resists and moves to add those teachers to his own group, Mr. Mead should continue to seek others who will work with him. Mr. Mead has the ability to bolster the library media center's curriculum involvement. He should find a way around Mr. Snyder's narrow view or a way out of the school (which might prove to be the best move for Mr. Mead). *(JM)*

GIVE IT SOME TIME

If Mr. Mead is "locked into" this school media program and cannot move to another school system or school building, he can seek the role of one who develops lesson plans for possible library activities and submits them to the head librarian. He could demonstrate support for the head librarian by helping him enhance some of the activities the head librarian started. In time, Mr. Mead may be accepted as a peer. This, however, is probably the least effective approach he could take. If there is no positive move on the part of the head librarian to support Mr. Mead as a peer in the instructional design process, he should seek another position. If no library media specialist positions become available, Mr. Mead might consider moving into the classroom and establishing himself as a teacher who generates library activities in support of his own lesson plans.

Of all the "resources" found in the school library media program, the professional media specialist is the most expensive and the most critical. Wasted talent and territorial struggles are two problems that can destroy any efforts to establish the school media program as the center for curriculum development. *(DC)*

BIBLIOGRAPHY

Chisholm, Margaret E., and Donald P. Ely. *Media Personnel in Education.* Englewood Cliffs, NJ: Prentice-Hall, 1976.
This is a detailed look at the many possible competencies of the district-level and building-level school media staff. Although based on the competencies often given in national and state standards of the 1960s and 1970s, this book will clearly show that there are plenty of professional responsibilities for more than one media specialist in the same building.

A further definition of these professional roles for the 1980s can be found in the new AASL/AECT guidelines, *Information Power.*

Murphy, Marcy. "Setting Goals for Organizational and Individual Achievement: An Overview." *Journal of Library Administration* 8(2) (1987): 65–80.

This review provides the basis for considerations which should be made by any professional who wants to set his or her own goals for achievement. Such written statements for performance goals might help in the communication process between two individuals who find they are in conflict concerning the division of responsibilities.

Prostano, Emanuel T., and Joyce S. Prostano. *The School Library Media Center.* Littleton, CO: Libraries Unlimited, 1987.

Chapter 5, "Personnel," provides several helpful job descriptions and defines specific differences in the roles of the principal, supervisor of media services, head of the school library, media technicians, and clerical staff.

Stueart, Robert D., and John Taylor Eastlick. *Library Management.* Littleton, CO: Libraries Unlimited, 1981.

Chapter 5, "Directing," provides a look at several management philosophies which should be considered as one determines a solution to the posed problems in Case 15. Other sections of this chapter deal with motivation, leadership, and communication.

White, Herbert S. *Library Personnel Management.* White Plains, NY: Knowledge Industry Publications, 1985.

Chapter 5, "Leadership, Supervision and the Decision Process," is worth reading to gain some insights into how to meet the problems posed in Case 15. Subtopics in this chapter include "When Supervisors Fail to Lead," "Leadership Traits," and "Sources of Authority."

Part II
Managing Resources and Equipment for Greater Access to Information

Case 16: Video Copyright Policies

Description

Prairie Highland is a rural school district with 1,800 students housed in three buildings on one campus. One library media specialist and three aides administer the library media program. Last year federal ESEA Chapter 2 funds were used to purchase a satellite dish. Programs from 92 stations, including one French Canadian and one Mexican, are now available for Prairie Highland's classrooms. The cultural advantage of hearing authentic French and Spanish spoken and the excellent science, nature, and literature programs on cable have been a boon for this small country district. Before approving the application for the satellite dish purchase, the state education agency was assured by the media specialist that the district would abide by the copyright law and rules given in the state guidelines when utilizing the programs taped from the air.

The media specialist has been rigorous in her efforts to comply. She went over the law with all teachers at an inservice day. Reminders of the copyright law are printed and kept with all video recorders and are handed out with blank tapes. Complete records are kept for all tapes recorded by the media center or on media center equipment so time limits can be observed and tapes erased on schedule.

Walking through the social studies hall one morning, the media specialist notices a teacher using a videotape of a network special that she thought had been erased several months ago. Confronted, the social studies teacher admits he copied the program at home on his own video recorder. Angrily he tells the media specialist to mind her own business, stating that since he buys his own tapes, uses his own equipment, and maintains his own collection, he has a right to anything he feels will be useful for his classes. He also tells her that he's not the only one making copies to keep. When reminded that he's breaking the law, the social studies teacher says it's for the good of education since Prairie Highland can't afford to buy the rights to these programs and students need them longer than the time allowed by law. "Besides, Prairie Highland is so far out in the country and so small no lawsuit would ever be filed against the district."

What options does the media specialist have to:

a. Enforce the district rules set up for use of the satellite dish hookup?
b. Bring this violation of the law to the attention of:
   1. The principal?
   2. The school board?
   3. The state education agency?
   4. Any other interested party, such as the network itself?

Response

INFORM THE ADMINISTRATION OF VIOLATION

The media specialist may remind the teacher that the state education agency granted permission to the school district to purchase the satellite dish on condition that the district abide by the copyright law and the rules given in the state guidelines when utilizing programs taped from the air.

She may offer to write to the network requesting permission to use the tape. Often a special license will be granted, allowing use of programs for educational purposes. Also, point out to the teacher that, as an instructor in the field of social studies, he is particularly obligated to teach respect for law and the importance of due process. The students might enjoy writing the letter of request. They might be quite surprised to learn that copyright is embedded in the principles of the Constitution.

If this discussion fails and the teacher remains angry, the library media specialist will have to tell him that, under the terms granting permission to the district to purchase the satellite dish, she has no recourse but to call the violation to the principal's attention. *(MO)*

CONTRARY TO PROFESSIONAL ETHICS

To begin, there are two questions that should be answered: (1) What is the district board's position on copyright compliance, and (2) is the board's position expressed in a written policy statement? (See figures 9 and 10 for sample copyright policies.)

There is some ambiguity regarding the teacher's position. Does he sincerely believe he has the legal right to use the recording in this manner, or does he know he is in violation of federal law but chooses to proceed anyway?

Figure 9. Sample Copyright Policy—Carmel Clay Schools

It is the intent of the Board of Education of Carmel Clay Schools to adhere to the provisions of the current copyright laws and Congressional guidelines.

The board recognizes that unlawful copying and use of copyrighted materials contributes to higher costs for materials, lessens the incentives for development of quality educational materials, and fosters an attitude of disrespect for law which is in conflict with the educational goals of this School Corporation.

The Board directs that Corporation employees adhere to all provisions of Title 17 of the United States Code, entitled "Copyrights," and other relative federal legislation and guidelines related to the duplication, retention, and use of copyrighted materials.

The Board further directs that:

1. Unlawful copies of copyrighted materials may not be produced on Corporation-owned equipment.
2. Unlawful copies of copyrighted materials may not be used with Corporation-owned equipment, within Corporation-owned facilities, or at Corporation-sponsored functions.
3. The legal and/or insurance protection of the Corporation will not be extended to employees who unlawfully copy and use copyrighted materials.

Employees who make and/or use copies of copyrighted materials in their jobs are expected to be familiar with published provisions regarding fair use and public display, and are further expected to be able to provide their supervisor, upon request, the justification under Sections 107 or 110 of USC 17 for copies that have been made or used.

Employees who use copyrighted materials which do not fall within fair use or public display guidelines will be able to substantiate that the materials meet one of the following tests:

1. The materials have been purchased from an authorized vendor by the individual employee or the Corporation and a record of the purchase exists.
2. The materials are copies covered by a licensing agreement between the copyright owner and the Corporation or the individual employee.
3. The materials are being reviewed or demonstrated by the user to reach a decision about possible future purchase or licensing and a valid agreement exists which allows for such use.

Though there continues to be controversy regarding interpretation of the copyright laws, this policy represents a sincere effort to operate legally. All school employees will be provided with copies of this policy and accompanying rulings.

Guidelines for Use of Copyrighted Materials

Copyright is the exclusive right that protects an author, composer, or programmer from having his or her work published, recorded, exhibited, translated, or reproduced by way of copies and other versions, except by permission. The purpose of copyright is to encourage the development of new and original works and to stimulate their wide distribution by assuring that their creators will be fairly compensated for their contributions to society.

Current American copyright law is embodied in Title 17 of the *United States Code.* Works of authorship include, but are not limited to, the following categories: computer programs; dramatic works, including any accompanying music; literary works; motion pictures and other audiovisual works; musical works, including any accompanying words; pantomimes and choreographic works; pictorial, graphic, and sculptural works; and sound recordings.

The law affects classroom practices and necessitates that educational staff examine:

—*What* they copy
—*How much* they copy
—The *purposes* for which they copy
—The *conditions* under which they copy

Of special interest to educational staff are the "fair use" doctrine and the accompanying Congressional guidelines which stipulate what may and may not be copied for use in schools and classrooms.

The following pages explain some highlights of the law and its accompanying guidelines. The guidelines, while not law, were generated in response to questions. They will be modified by future court decisions and legislative action. However, they are an interpretation of the law as developed by Congressional subcommittees.

Videotapes

Recording Television Broadcasts
The guidelines were developed to apply only to off-air recording by nonprofit educational institutions:

An individual teacher may:

...record a broadcast program off-air simultaneously with broadcast transmission (including simultaneous cable retransmission) and retain it for a period *not to exceed the first forty-five (45) consecutive calendar days* after the date of recording. Upon conclusion of such retention period, all off-air recordings must be erased or destroyed immediately. "Broadcast programs" are television programs transmitted by television stations for reception by the general public without charge.

...use off-air recordings once in the course of relevant teaching activities, and repeated once only when instructional reinforcement is necessary, in classrooms and similar places devoted to instruction within a single building, cluster, or campus, as well as in the homes of students receiving formalized home instruction, during the first 10 consecutive school days in the 45 calendar-day retention period. "School days" are school session days—not counting weekends, holidays, vacations, examination periods, or other scheduled interruptions—within the 45 calendar day retention period.

...make off-air recordings only at the request of and for use by individual teachers. Off-air recordings may not be regularly recorded in anticipation of requests. No broadcast program may be recorded off-air more than once at the request of the same teacher, regardless of the number of times the program may be broadcast.

...reproduce a limited number of copies from each off-air recording to meet the legitimate needs of teachers under these guidelines. Each such additional copy shall be subject to all provisions governing the original recording.

...after the first 10 consecutive school days, use off-air recordings to the end of the 45-calendar-day retention period only for teacher evaluation purposes, i.e., to determine whether or not to include the broadcast program in the teaching curriculum. The recording may not be used in the recording institution for student exhibition or any other nonevaluative purpose without authorization.

...use only a portion of an off-air recording. Off-air programs need not be used in their entirety, but the recorded programs may not be altered from their original content. Off-air recordings may not be physically or electronically combined or merged to constitute teaching anthologies or compilations.

Note: All copies of off-air recordings must include the copyright notice on the broadcast program as recorded.

Each school is expected to establish appropriate control procedures to maintain the integrity of these guidelines.

In January 1984, the U.S. Supreme Court ruled, in the so-called SONY Betamax case, that the videotaping of television programs off the air for home use is not a violation of copyright law. Some educators contend that the Court said it is now all right for a teacher to tape any program at home, carry it to school, and use it in the classroom. "Anyone who thinks this is making a grave mistake," says Kenton Pattie, who heads the Government Relations Department of the International Communications Industries Association. "There is absolutely nothing in the 82-page decision to support this contention." Carmel Clay Schools is accepting the Senate Committee Guidelines that a program *may be taped at home or school* for use, *but played only once,* plus one time for reinforcement. *Permission to retain and use again,* however, must be obtained from the copyright holder.

USING COPYRIGHTED VIDEOTAPES

A teacher may:

...use in face-to-face instruction a videocassette *purchased by the school* even though it bears a warning label "For Home Use Only." The key is that the tape is *incorporated as part of the systematic teaching* activities of the program in which it is being used.

...use for instructional purposes a *rental videocassette* bearing the "For Home Use Only" label if the school has obtained a release statement from the rental agency granting permission for instructional use of the program. (The release statement is available in the media center.)

A teacher may not:

...use either a purchased or rental video program labeled "For Home Use Only" in other than planned, direct, instructional activities. The program may *not* be used for entertainment, nor fund-raisers, nor time-fillers. Any use, other than instructional, must be negotiated at the time of purchase or rental, usually in the form of a licensing agreement.

...make an archival or backup copy of a copyrighted film or videotape.

Figure 10. Sample Copyright Policy—Fort Wayne Community Schools

Fort Wayne Community School Media Services Department
(Fort Wayne, Indiana)

TO: Middle School Principals

FROM: Lavon Hart, Supervisor of Audiovisual
Communications

RE: Videotaping Policy

DATE: 10/17/84

After much discussion with Middle School Media Teachers and Principals, the following concerns have been expressed relative to videotape recordings:

1. There is a general feeling among teachers that they can request "any" off-air program to be taped and retained for any length of time regardless of the copyright laws.
2. Many programs are poorly used in the classroom by the teaching staff. This "strain" on the few existing video cassette recorders prevents the conscientious teacher from utilizing appropriate programs.
3. The lack of a consistent policy for recording and use of videotape recordings places the Media Teacher in the middle of ethical practice and peer teacher pressure.

With these concerns in mind, the following videotape policy is to be put in effect after your approval:

Videotaping Policy

This policy for videotaping television programs off-air is to be followed at the FWCS Middle Schools.

1. The FWCS Media Services Department supports the "Guidelines for Off-Air Recording of Broadcast Programming for Educational Purposes" as presented to the Congressional Copyright Committee and as read into the *Congressional Record.*
2. Before any off-air television program will be videotaped, it must be requested, in writing, by a staff member of the school. The request shall be submitted on the *FWCS VIDEO-TAPING REQUEST AND STATEMENT OF POLICY* form.
   a. Use of the form will notify the staff that consideration must be given to the legal use of off-air programs.
   b. Use of the form will protect the FWCS, as a system, from potential copyright violation lawsuits.

    c. Use of the form will inform teachers that proper steps will be taken to legally provide (within reason) appropriate programming for class use.

    d. Use of the form will provide a written release to remove the Media Teacher and/or his assigns from any legal suits inasmuch as videotaping services are provided at the formal request of a teacher or administrator (as provided in the copyright law).

3. If the program needs to be retained beyond the normal use period, the *REQUEST FOR TELEVISION VIDEO-TAPE RETENTION* form will be completed [Authors' note: See Figure 11]. The building principal will indicate support of the request by signing the form. The form will then be put with the videotape and submitted to the Media Services Department for action. A good tape will be returned to the school for re-use. If acceptance by the copyright holder is given, the tape will then be kept in the FWCS Media Library. The final decision to keep the tape will be based on the following:

    a. Cost of the program

    b. Availability of funds

    c. Curricular integration possibilities

    d. Potential of the number of schools to use the program

    e. Long-term viability of the program

    f. Whether up-to-date media is already available in the school's or Media Library collection.

4. The department heads should be encouraged to "weed" any existing videotape collection to meet the previously stated guidelines.

Potential Questions from Staff

a. Question: What do we do with the existing tapes in each building?
Answer: Have department heads "weed" out unnecessary ones. Begin retention procedures for the rest of them.

b. Question: Who decides what ones are to be kept?
Answer: The Media Teacher will contact each Department Head (if needed) and generate a "need to keep" priority list. This list will be sent to Mr. Hart. The list will be reviewed and recommendations will be made.

c. Question: How do we get permission to retain them?
Answer: From the aforementioned list, permission to retain will be sought from the copyright holder by the Media Services Department.

d. Question: Who obtains the rights?
   Answer: If permission is granted, the approval will be kept on file in the Media Service Department, and the tape will be sent to the Media Library for inclusion in the collection.

e. Question: Who pays for the retention rights?
   Answer: If payment is necessary for retention, appropriate action will be taken to obtain funding.

f. Question: Where will the tapes be kept?
   Answer: All tapes, approved for retention, will be housed in the FWCS Media Library. Access to them will be by normal requesting procedures for *all* media from the collection.

g. Question: If a teacher makes a tape at home and brings it to school to be used over the T.V. Distribution System, what do we do?
   Answer: If the teacher made the request to tape it, and you were unable to comply due to conflicts of time or equipment, they may copy it at home and bring it to school for use, following normal procedures.

h. Question: If a teacher buys, borrows, or rents a prerecorded tape which is specified by the copyright holder, producer or supplier as being for *Home Use Only*, can it be used in the classroom?
   Answer: Yes! With the following conditions ...
   1. The tape must be a legitimate copy.
   2. The tape is to be shown in a classroom or similar place devoted to instruction.
   3. The performance on the tape must be for a course of instruction and not for entertainment, recreation, or cultural value.
   4. The tape must be played in the classroom and not transmitted on a closed-circuit television system.
   5. Attendance at the showing is limited to the instructor, pupils and guest lecturers. (Classes are not to be grouped together for a single showing.)

Instructional Reasons for Videotaping a Television Program

Important Reasons
   a. To extend the range of experiences available to students
   b. To present new information
   c. To provide a different approach for presenting the same material
   d. To reinforce material taught in other lessons
   e. To bring new resources and/or persons into the classroom (resources *not available* from other FWCS sources)

f. To motivate students' interest in a subject

g. To permit individualization of instruction

h. To serve as a suitable teaching alternative in emergency situations (e.g. long-term teacher absence)

i. To delay viewing since the broadcast schedule is not convenient

j. To determine whether the program is appropriate for future class use

Not Important

a. To lighten the teacher load

b. To allow the teacher to observe the students

c. To allow the teacher and/or students a time to relax

d. Because students like TV

Reprinted with permission from Fort Wayne Community Schools, Fort Wayne, IN.

If the former is the case, the teacher is incorrect. Section 106 of Title 17 of the *United States Code,* titled *Copyrights,* makes clear that the right "to reproduce the copyrighted work" is exclusive to the copyright owner. None of the possible exceptions to that exclusive right cited in sections 107 through 118 of the *Code* applies to the situation described in this case. The 1984 Supreme Court decision in the so-called SONY Betamax case, which ruled that videotaping programs off the air at home for private use is not a violation of copyright law, does not apply here. The Court used the phrase "private home use" several times in its decision, leaving no room to argue that tapes recorded off the air at home can be arbitrarily converted to school use. The law says *private*—meaning to show to immediate family or to an informal gathering of close friends.

If the latter is the case, the teacher is behaving in a manner so contrary to accepted professional ethics as to warrant dismissal. That a professional educator would teach his or her students, by example, that it is perfectly acceptable to violate the law on such insupportable grounds as "everyone else is doing it" or "I don't expect to get caught" is unconscionable. In a different regard, it is extremely unprofessional of the teacher to place the school district in a position of such vulnerability, opening the possibility of prosecution in the federal courts. If the district cannot afford to pay programming licenses, it certainly cannot afford to pay fines and damages. *(JWS)*

ESTABLISH POLICY AND COMMUNICATE

The first step that should be taken to help remedy this situation is to develop a systemwide copyright policy that conforms to the nationally accepted copyright guidelines and laws. Ideally, the policy

Figure 11. Sample Videotape Request Form

REQUEST FOR TELEVISION VIDEO TAPE RETENTION

TO: FWCS Media Services Department
    Supervisor of Audio Visual Communications

FROM: School_____

      Media Teacher_____

      Requesting Teacher_____

DATE: _____

We do hereby request that the copyright holders of the following television program be contacted relative to obtaining permission to use a video tape copy in the Fort Wayne Community Schools.

Name of program_____

Date of telecast_____Channel of telecast_____

Length of telecast_____Course of study_____

                    Requesting Teacher Signature_____

                    Principal Approval_____

For Media Services Department Use Only:

Name of Producer_____

Network Affiliation_____

  Request sent: Date_____

  Answer received: Date_____

Cost of program_____

NOTES:

This program has been: ☐ *approved*
                        ☐ *disapproved*
for retention and circulation by the FWCS Media Library.

Date_____ Initial_____

Reason for Disapproval:

☐ Copyright holder will not give permission.

☐ Cannot find copyright holder.

☐ Program cost prohibitive.

☐ Sufficient funds not available at this time.

☐ Similar media available from Media Library.

☐ Potential curricular use of programs insufficient to warrant purchase.

☐ Content will become out-dated very soon.

☐ Other_____

Reprinted with permission from Fort Wayne Community Schools, Fort Wayne, IN.

should be developed by a committee consisting of the media specialist, faculty representatives from each building, and administrative representatives.

The media specialist's role should not be that of a police officer. She should continue to videotape and use equipment only in accordance with the copyright policy and to support that policy by word and deed at all times.

An effort should be made to make moneys available to purchase or lease rights for those programs that teachers feel would be a valuable addition to the permanent media collection. If teachers know that the media specialist is making every effort to support their needs, she will probably discover that they will become more cooperative in helping her to follow the copyright policy. *(JJ)*

BIBLIOGRAPHY

American Association of School Librarians and Association for Educational Communications and Technology. *Information Power: Guidelines for School Library Media Programs.* Chicago: American Library Association, 1988.
See pages 5–6, 98. "In all cases, library media specialists must adhere to and promote the legal and ethical use of copyrighted materials. The protection and recognition of the rights of the copyright holder will ensure continued development of quality instructional materials."

Bender, Ivan R. "Copyright Law and Educational Media." Library Trends 34(1) (1985): 95–110.
Bender attempts to review sections of copyright laws that are most relevant to media librarians. Discussion includes Public Law 94-553, the BOCES case (1977), and the SONY case (1976).

———. "The Legal Copy." *TLC Guide* (1984–present).
Since 1984 this has been a regular column in this guide to educational television. Bender is an attorney who served on the committee that negotiated the guidelines for off-air videotaping. The *TLC Guide* is published for schools and libraries seven times during the school year. *Contact:* Television Licensing Center, 5547 North Ravenswood Ave., Chicago, IL 60640; 1-(800)-323-4222 or 1-(312)-878-2600.

"Copyright, Media, and the School Librarian." *School Media Quarterly* 6(3) (1978): 192A–92P.
A special guide developed by the American Association of School Librarians which raises several questions concerning when it may or may not be legal to copy materials. Although some of the information in now dated, it covers a wide variety of media and situations including those times when a student may copy materials for educational purposes.

Ernst, Wanna. "Censorship: An Overview of What Is Happening in School Library Media Centers and Other Areas of Education." *School Library Media Annual 1985.* Edited by Shirley L. Aaron and Pat R. Scales, pp. 9–36. Littleton, CO: Libraries Unlimited, 1985.

Probably the most recent comprehensive discussion on censorship in the schools. One section includes "self-censorship by school librarians, teachers, and administrators."

Flygare, Thomas J. "Photocopying and Videotaping for Educational Purposes: The Doctrine of Fair Use." *Phi Delta Kappan* 65(8) (1984): 568–69.
A review of the 1981 House Judiciary Committee guidelines. Reference is given to the 1984 *SONY Corporation vs. Universal Studios* case. Flygare has written extensively concerning many legal issues in education.

Helm, Virginia M. *What Educators Should Know about Copyright* (Fastback 233). Bloomington, IN: Phi Delta Kappa Educational Foundation, 1986.
A clear guide to many copyright issues. In direct and easy to understand terms, responsibilities and possible penalties are given. This inexpensive (90 cents) booklet covers a wide range of topics from computers to video, from Supreme Court decisions to fair use statutory factors, from home use only to live transmitted performances.

Logan, Elisabeth. "Copyright and New Technology." In *School Library Media Annual 1987.* Edited by Shirley Aaron and Pat R. Scales, pp. 32–43. Littleton, CO: Libraries Unlimited, 1987.
Updates guidelines for off-air videotaping from publicly available television programs.

Magaro, John D. "Guidelines for Off-Air Copying." 1982. ERIC document ED 234 775.
Gives full guidelines developed by a special committee appointed by Congressman Robert Kastenmeier.

Martin, Elizabeth. "Basic Copyright Concerns: A Guide for Library Media Specialists." In *School Library Media Annual 1985.* Edited by Shirley L. Aaron and Pat R. Scales, pp. 44–56. Littleton, CO: Libraries Unlimited, 1985.
Of special value in this review of the copyright issue are several guides which outline the minimum standards for educational fair use.

Niemeyer, Karen K. "Copyright and Technology." In *School Library Media Annual 1986.* Edited by Shirley Aaron and Pat R. Scales, pp. 22–42. Littleton, CO: Libraries Unlimited, 1986.
Provides an easy-to-follow listing of what a "teacher may and may not do" within the copyright guidelines.

Pemberton, J. Michael. *Policies of Audiovisual Producers and Distributors: A Handbook for Acquisition Personnel.* Metuchen, NJ: Scarecrow Press, 1984.
Addresses the policies of several hundred major producers of educational film and video programs. This useful handbook will indicate if the producer or distributor of the product will grant permission for duplication of video recordings, although such permission should be gained in written form before actual duplication takes place.

Reed, Mary Hutchings, and Debra Stanek. "Library and Classroom Use of Copyrighted Videotapes and Computer Software." *American Libraries* 17(2) (1986): 120 A–D Insert.
    A point-by-point summary of the application of the Copyright Revision Act of 1976 to educational uses of commercial video programs. Applications to computer software are also noted.

Sinofsky, Esther R. *Off-Air Videotaping in Education: Copyright Issues, Decisions, Implications.* New York: R.R. Bowker Company, 1984.
    An extensive discussion of copyright issues related to television programming. Of specific use is the chapter that deals with potential solutions and outlines the process of gaining permission or "licensing" to copy educational programs.

Troost, F. William. "A Practical Guide to Dealing with Copyright Problems Related to Emerging Video Technologies in the Schools and Colleges." *Library Trends* 32(2) (1983): 211–21.
    Application of the copyright guidelines to daily activities and policy of the media center is described. "Permission-to-Use" request forms are provided. This entire issue is devoted to "current problems in copyright" and includes articles by the following who have written extensively on the topic: Walter Allen, Roger Billings, Nancy H. Marshall, and Jerome K. Miller.

Case 17: Equipment Depreciation

Description

Addison Community Schools is a suburban system of 9,586 students. After several years of stagnation, the student population has begun to grow again, and a closed elementary is being refurbished to reopen next fall. There are six other elementaries, two middle schools, and two high schools. Ages of the buildings vary from 10 to 25 years. Each high school has two library media specialists, and the other schools have one professional media person. There are no aides, but a strong volunteer program makes adult help available to all media centers. There is no district-level library media supervisor. The curriculum director and the finance officer direct the program and fiscal development aspects for the media specialists.

The associate superintendent for finance has been with the district for over 30 years and will retire in 4 more. He has kept this school system solvent through good times and bad. There has never been a line item for replacement of audiovisual equipment in his budget. He is adamant in his feeling that there is no need for this expense, and since his method has worked over the years, he is not interested in change. Equipment was purchased for each school from capital funds when buildings were constructed.

This year has seen a crisis in those schools that are 15 years old and older. Much of the equipment is beyond repair, and increased complaints from teachers have made the situation so desperate that a million-dollar bond issue will be on the next local ballot. It will provide money to replace worn-out equipment in all schools as well as complete the purchase of the computer hardware needed for the district's long-range computer programs. The financial officer has said he plans to purchase equipment that will last at least 20 years.

The head media specialist at Addison Central High School had the most trouble and worry from her staff, as ACHS is the oldest building with the oldest equipment. She is excited at the prospect of having everything new but feels strongly that some reasonable depreciation schedule to maintain and replace equipment should be set by the district. The head media specialist would like to convince the administration to look at equipment standards used in other districts and consider unique needs in each building rather than an arbitrary time line.

If you were the head media specialist at Addison Central High School:

   a. What evidence could you present to the central administration to prove your point that the district should depreciate equipment on a regular schedule?

   b. What argument could you make for and against the purchase of all new equipment every 20 years?

   c. What might you do to generate support for your plans with others in the community?

Response

DEPRECIATION APPLIES TO BUSINESS, NOT EDUCATION

Since your scenario does not allow for a line item for equipment replacement, I will assume that there is a line item for contracted services sufficient to maintain the equipment that does exist. Until replacement parts become unavailable for a particular model of equipment, anything can be fixed when it breaks. The greater question is when is enough repair enough? The media specialist should maintain service records on each piece of equipment to document the service activity and the cost of the service to maintain the equipment. These service records should make a very strong case to any administrator of the need to have a line item for equipment replacement. I generally declare something salvage when the cost of repair exceeds 75% of the replacement value. In the case of your scenario, the media specialist would have no other option than to use the contracted services account to pay for repairs in excess of the replacement value since there is no replacement for vitally needed equipment. I would fault the media specialist who would knowingly allow the building's equipment to fall into such disrepair that it is beyond hope.

I would not totally agree with a set depreciation schedule for equipment. A depreciation schedule is a management technique in business dealing with tax incentives and tax write-offs. In the school setting, there are none of the same incentives and a set depreciation schedule of 5 or 7 years really has no meaning. I would, however, favor a policy that would allow the replacement of equipment when a certain set of factors "kick in." Some of the factors could be age, repair vs. replacement costs, newer versions or formats of equipment that make it obsolete, time involved in repairs, reliability of the company, excessive repairs as indicated by the service records that are maintained, or electronics that are difficult to maintain. A fairly simple machine such as a filmstrip projector may operate for years without even simple maintenance, while other items such as a cheap tape recorder could be declared salvage in a single year if the motor fails.

An additional factor would be a maintenance schedule for some of the more complex equipment. I have in mind 16mm projectors, video equipment, and computers. As a matter of routine, these items should be serviced yearly on a set schedule to ensure that your scenario of a desperate situation does not occur, and so that someone with technical knowledge can evaluate the equipment and complaints.

For the final question of buying equipment every 20 years, that premise is a false economy from its inception. Given the very best of circumstances, only a limited number of items on the market today could be expected to last 20 years. Without serious consideration being given to a maintenance routine, many pieces of equipment will not last past the first 5 years and the desperate situation will recur. *(REW)*

IMPORTANCE OF LOCAL MAINTENANCE

First-level maintenance occurs at the local school media center and encompasses the following: replacing projection lamps, keeping equipment clean, and performing other preventative maintenance. The second level of maintenance is the district repair department. Second-level repairs include directly replacing parts of the mechanical and/or electronic system; cleaning the equipment internally and externally and doing routine preventative maintenance; and lubricating and adjusting the equipment, including alignment.

Third-level maintenance is the most critical in cost justification. This is done at a repair center different from the school district's repair department.

It can be shown with repair records that in schools where a routine preventative maintenance schedule is established and followed by media personnel and/or trained students, there is a significant decrease in repair costs. *(LH)*

BIBLIOGRAPHY

American Association of School Librarians and Association for Educational Communications and Technology. *Information Power: Guidelines for School Library Media Programs.* Chicago: American Library Association, 1988.

See pages 70–79, 82, 127. "Further technological developments are likely to occur, necessitating a continuous evaluation of new information systems for access, production, storage, and delivery in order to assess their potential benefits to teachers and students."

Crowe, Virginia. "Choosing Technologies for School Library Media Centers: Hardware Selection." *Drexel Library Quarterly* 20(1) (1984): 51–63.
A clear outline of selection criteria along with advice on "writing specifications," and "bidding procedures."

"Feedback (and Lack Thereof)." *EPIEgram Equipment* 13(3) (1984): 1–3.
Describes the problems in determining the longevity or life span of audiovisual equipment. "Average life in hours" is given for categories of common AV equipment.

Kalmbach, John A., and Richard D. Kruzel. "Buying and Maintaining Audio-Visual Equipment. *Media & Methods* 25 (3) (1989): 9–15.
Building a close professional relationship with a local dealer is emphasized. Information gained through attending workshops and conferences on new equipment may be more useful than waiting for evaluations through printed review sources.

Post, Richard. "Longevity and Depreciation of Audiovisual Equipment." *Tech Trends* 32(6) (1987): 12–24.
Data are presented from the Inter-University Council of Media Educators which will give the school library media specialist some idea of the normal longevity of common pieces of audiovisual equipment. Sample depreciation calculations are also provided.

Schmid, William T. *Media Center Management.* New York: Hastings, 1980.
In chapter 5, "Cost Accounting," Schmid gives examples of a depreciation inventory for media center equipment.

Case 18: A Donation from a Board Member

Description ———————————————

Harold Murry, the head media specialist for Taft High School, receives a telephone call from Dr. Marvin Mullins, a member of the school board. Dr. Mullins is a successful dentist and a twice unsuccessful candidate for U.S. Congress, losing both times in the primary election.

Dr. Mullins informs Mr. Murry that he has just discussed with the Taft High School principal the idea of donating a subscription of a national weekly newspaper to the school library. Dr. Mullins states that not only has the principal approved of the idea, but that the media specialist at the other high school welcomes the idea, too. Although Mr. Murry is not sure, he seems to remember the newspaper as having a very clear conservative bias.

"Of course," says Dr. Mullins, "the paper can be used in any manner you and your teachers see fit. I'll just pay for a year's subscription beginning next week."

Currently the media center receives two newspapers: the local daily paper and a daily paper from a large city just a 30-minute drive to the north. Both papers are held for 2 weeks and then discarded. There is no attempt to clip the papers for vertical-file materials.

As Mr. Murry, consider the following:

a. How do you respond to Dr. Mullins?
b. What purpose might a collection development policy serve in this situation?

Response

ESTABLISH POLICY

Mr. Murry must express appreciation for the thoughtful gesture, taking care not to extend that gratitude to the receipt of the newspaper itself. If the district does not have a collection development policy that includes both a statement relevant to gifts and a "Donation Agreement" form, this may not be the most appropriate time to instigate such a procedure. It may be less controversial to wait until the subscription expires or Dr. Mullins is no longer on the board, whichever happens first. If, on the other hand, such a gift policy now exists, Mr. Murry must call this to the attention of the principal and solicit the principal's help in focusing the attention of other administrators on it. In either case he needs to visit with the principal to discuss the policy (or the lack of it) and his need to be consulted about the acceptance of gifts for the media center.

After Mr. Murry receives the paper and has had an opportunity to evaluate its contents, he has the option to make it available or to throw it away—either alternative can put him at risk. Because of the potentially volatile circumstances, Mr. Murry needs to inform the principal of his decision with justifications for his judgment. He should not be intimidated because the donor is a board member, is a citizen with professional status, and has political aspirations.

High school students need access to more than two newspapers; perhaps Mr. Murry could suggest the title of a more objective paper and ask Dr. Mullins if he would be interested in substituting subscriptions. Apparently funds are tight in Mr. Murry's school. If such practices by donors are (or may become) a recurring problem, it might be wise to develop a list of well-identified materials and equipment needed in the library, make the list available to administrators, and suggest that nonmonetary gifts conform to the list. *(AH)*

USE SAME CRITERIA

Most policy statements concerning gifts indicate that the librarian will make a judgment about the merits of the gift on the basis of the same criteria used to purchase materials. Unless the newspaper is clearly slanted or bias, *and* clearly would be of no benefit to the academic exercises of the school, it would be unlikely one could deny acceptance of the subscription. The school library media specialist could consider a subscription to a newspaper that reflects the other extreme of the political pole in order to "balance" the collection, but such investment would probably not be worthwhile unless assignments from social studies teachers, for example, call for gathering various editorial opinions on current national and world issues. If the donated newspaper is one of national stature and has a reputation for being "factual" if not always objective, then it would be difficult to envision a selection policy that would prevent such a gift from becoming part of the collection. *(AH)*

BIBLIOGRAPHY

Adams, Helen R. *School Media Policy Development.* Littleton, CO: Libraries Unlimited, 1986.
Adams provides an excellent framework for involving members of the board of education in the policy-writing process. Through this process, board members may become more aware of the selection process and the need to balance the collection.

Kemp, Betty. *School Library and Media Center Acquisitions Policies and Procedures.* Phoenix, AZ: Oryx Press, 1986.
Several examples of policy statements are provided. "Acceptance of gifts will be determined by the library media specialist on the basis of their suitability to the library media center's purposes and needs. . . ." Examples of policy statements concerning selection of "free" materials are also given.

Case 19: You Can't Weed

Description

Janie Wallace has taken her first job as a school media specialist. She follows a school librarian who had been with Lakeview Junior High School for 23 years. During her first semester, Ms. Wallace discovers many titles in the book collection that she feels are out of date and should not be available to students. Many of the materials in the science area, for example, date before any manned spaceflights. There is still shelving for additional books, and many of the materials also are too worn and unattractive for the students to select.

Not only is the book collection in need of attention, but the sound filmstrip collection also seems to be very dated. Some filmstrip kits have not been used for over 5 years. Teachers who have used the kits in the past tell her they now use other materials because the filmstrips are no longer relevant to what they do in the classroom. A few teachers indicate the desire to use more video programs, if only there were more pieces of equipment and more money to invest in such materials. There is no space to store additional videos.

When she proposes to the principal the need to weed the collection, Ms. Wallace is informed that the materials are public property and should not be discarded. In addition, the principal informs her, "We have just enough books to be over the minimum number per student required by the state and certification standards. If we get rid of any, we fall below the guidelines."

Ms. Wallace knows that other schools have allowed weeding, and, indeed, often encouraged it. Books are removed from the shelves and replaced with more attractive and current materials. Old books are sold to raise part of the money to purchase new titles.

Ms. Wallace has also determined that her book budget is rather low in comparison to the neighboring school districts. She wonders if the budget will remain that way as long as the administration feels there is no need to expand the collection.

What can Ms. Wallace do to:

a. Demonstrate that materials need to be removed and replaced?
b. Show what effect new materials might have on teacher and student use of the library?
c. Involve teachers in both the weeding and materials selection processes?
d. Establish a systematic plan for continuous evaluation of the collection?

Response

BRING THE OUT-OF-DATE MATERIALS TO THE ATTENTION OF THE TEACHERS

To demonstrate the need to weed, as well as the positive effect of up-to-date materials, Ms. Wallace might develop bibliographies on selected topics of current interest. Ms. Wallace should talk with the English and social studies departments (or any staff who actively uses the library) about student reports that have been documented recently, or topics that might be researched in the near future. The bibliographies should show dates available from the current collection and point out flagrantly outdated facts or information, such as statistical data. At the same time, bibliographies from another school's collection should be prepared. She should also note in the bibliographies new materials available for purchase if only the money and space were present.

If there are teachers who are concerned about these problems, Ms. Wallace should enlist their help in talking with the administration. They could make presentations or complaints as individuals, as a department, or in a group of their own choosing. In many cases, the best way to call attention to a problem is to get a large group of people complaining about the same issue.

An informal poll of students might also be conducted through cooperative teachers. Questions should be geared to address the specific problem of outdated materials. Student recognition of the problem may help her case.

One of the best ways to involve staff in weeding as well as selection decisions is with a personal approach. As Ms. Wallace considers an area for weeding, she should ask individuals within that department for their help. She could explain what she is doing and how much she needs their subject expertise. Most will be happy to help.

Once a decision has been made about items to be weeded, Ms. Wallace should follow district policy on discarding items. In our district, items are not available for auction or sale because they were purchased with public moneys. First review goes to the faculty and staff in our building. While browsing through discards, the teachers may find items that should not be discarded, or items that may be of personal interest. After faculty members have been given their option, other district employees are notified about the materials. Final option is given to students in the school, and any remaining items are thrown away. Last year we pulled 1,000 nonfiction titles and threw away only 200 after this procedure was followed.

A similar method of staff involvement in selection can be used. As announcements of items come in (blurbs, flyers, or catalogs), Ms. Wallace could channel them to the appropriate staff member(s). She should help teachers locate or become aware of reviews of these items and ask for their opinion about purchase. If items are purchased, she should make sure to let staff members know, especially those who helped in the selection of materials.

To establish a long-range plan, Ms. Wallace should prepare a written statement concerning collection development and evaluation. Rationale should be provided and guidelines developed. Ms. Wallace might want to contact other librarians in her district or area for similar policies and ideas. *(VH)*

CITE SPECIFIC EXAMPLES

Ms. Wallace needs to make her case with her principal by bringing in specific examples. She should draw to the principal's attention an outdated science book with inaccurate and/or dated information, or any outdated and poor quality AV with specific reasons why these materials cannot be good sources of information for the students. She can certainly express her responsibility as a professional who wants to offer only accurate information and feels the obligation to withdraw outdated materials.

If Ms. Wallace is assisting her teachers, she can communicate how little she has that is up to date on the curriculum subject areas. She certainly can be straightforward about new materials she knows of, via recognized reviews, but has no funds to purchase. Suggestions that the teachers pass this information on to the building administrator are perfectly legitimate. As teachers become more and more aware of the good materials that are available, they will begin lobbying for those materials also.

Weeding should be done yearly during inventory if at no other time. I never seem to have sufficient time at the end of the year to inventory everything, so I do sections in rotation. As these books or other materials are checked, they are also examined for datedness and poor physical condition. Discarded materials in our state are to be shredded unless permission is granted for other use.

Ms. Wallace, and all library/media professionals, must continue to stress that quantity does not necessarily mean quality. *(MPD)*

WEEDING WILL INCREASE CIRCULATION

Janie Wallace could demonstrate the need to remove and replace materials by doing a study of a sample of items in circulation or on the shelves to show the last previous check-out date. The purpose of the study would be to determine, for example, that most of the items in the sample have not been checked out since August 1983. A further sample might help one discover that 65% of the items on the shelves were last checked out in that time period. From such samples she might project for the administrators that removing 35% of that collection will decrease circulation by no more than 5% and probably increase it because individual titles likely to be chosen would be easier to locate.

She could give a more direct demonstration by removing the items in one area of the collection that had not circulated in the last 3 years and comparing circulation before and after the weeding of the section. Items could be stored for possible reshelving to meet the "no-discarding" mandate.

Ms. Wallace could take the next logical step after her weeding demonstration by using a disproportionate share of the available funds to buy materials in the area weeded and check the circulation again. If it increased markedly, this would provide a useful demonstration of the value of weeding out the obsolete and offering the most recent materials possible.

Naturally, involving students and teachers in selection and weeding would tend to increase their interest and, therefore, their use of the collection. In "Weeding the Library Media Collection" (Iowa Department of Public Instruction, 1984), I proposed a combination of an objective sort using the last previous check-out date to flag items and a subjective evaluation by teachers first and then by the library media staff. Items would be pulled from the shelves and placed on a cart. Teachers would be supplied with flags to indicate recommendations to weed or to retain. Items marked to retain would be returned to the shelves. I strongly recommended that if you ask for the teachers' advice, you take it.

This would be an appropriate time to seek a teacher's advice on what areas need to be built up and what format would be most helpful. Teachers could be encouraged to share bibliographies in current texts and curriculum guides and could be supplied with reviews on cards prepared by library media staff, covering their subject area. They could be asked to indicate priority if all titles can't be purchased.

If the library media staff meets regularly with teachers to select texts or plan curriculum, there should be many opportunities to involve teachers in the weeding and selection related to the areas being covered.

"Weeding the Library Media Collection" concludes that:

> The most practical program for community college and school libraries would appear to be to establish a cycle, such as three years, weeding a part of the collection each year. This should be supplemented by incidental weeding related to selection and circulation. Combining the weeding and inventory processes may save steps.

In "Planning the School Library Media Center Budget" (Iowa Department of Public Instruction, 1984), I proposed maintenance components for a budget in realistic collection replacement cycles and demonstrated probable costs for 10-, 15-, and 20-year cycles.

Ms. Wallace should study the needs of the library she serves, the funds currently available, and the likelihood of increases if justification can be provided. She then needs to propose a specific weeding and replacement policy and a program for disposal of weeded items. If she does indeed propose white elephant sales, she needs to be sure these ghosts will not come back to haunt her. *(BJB)*

A PROFESSIONAL DETERMINES QUALITY

Presumably, Ms. Wallace was hired because of her expertise to perform professional functions, e.g., maintain a collection responsive to the needs of her clientele. Does Ms. Wallace need to ask if she can weed her collection anymore than the English teacher needs to ask if he or she can teach proper sentence structure? However, since Ms. Wallace did ask and received a negative response, her options are limited; she cannot weed the collection without defying authority, not a pleasant situation.

A major problem exists in that standards frequently tend to emphasize numbers. Education on many levels is needed to communicate the ethical responsibilities that educators have for providing accurate information to students who are not sufficiently mature to read critically and to carefully select reading/listening/viewing materials that are appropriate to their needs. Only well-focused, accurate, and aesthetically pleasing library collections can serve the demands implicit in educational programs committed to excellence. *(AH)*

BIBLIOGRAPHY

American Association of School Librarians and Association for Educational Communications and Technology. *Information Power: Guidelines for School Library Media Programs.* Chicago: American Library Association, 1988.
See pages 79–80. "Criteria for removing items are identified in the school's collection development plan and provide guidelines for evaluating physical deterioration, obsolescence, and appropriateness for the current needs of the school community."

Buckingham, Betty Jo. "Planning the School Library Media Center Budget." Iowa State Department of Public Instruction, 1984. ERIC document 242 324.
Buckingham presents guidelines for planning the budget based on both short- and long-range plans and the specific goals and objectives of the school district. A sample budget is provided.

———. "Weeding." *Indiana Media Journal* 9(3) (1987): 19–25.
A step-by-step process is outlined. A sample circulation count chart is provided.

———. "Weeding the Library Media Collection." Iowa State Department of Public Instruction, 1984. ERIC document ED 253 240.
A thoughtful gathering of reasons why the librarian should weed and involve others in the process. Methods are outlined clearly and are based on successful experiences.

Calgary Board of Education. "Weeding the School Library Media Collection." *School Library Media Quarterly* 12(5) (1984): 419–24.
A clear and concise plan for weeding a school library collection. The school librarian will, however, want to question a few of the guidelines as to how they may or may not apply to his or her specific school.

Palmer, Roberta Gaetz. "A Practical Way to Weed Fiction in the School Library." *Principal* 67(3) (1988): 51–52.
Palmer gives special emphasis to required reading lists and materials that may be included in the school district's curriculum guide as important items to check before books are weeded from the library collection. In most cases, when a book title appears on a required reading list, duplicate copies should be purchased for the library.

Segel, Joseph P. *Evaluating and Weeding Collections in Small and Medium-Sized Public Libraries: The CREW Method.* Chicago: American Library Association, 1980.
An easy-to-understand weeding handbook which will give the industrious school librarian many ideas. Although tested in a public library setting, the method has many areas which transfer to school libraries. The school librarian will want to factor in the impact of the curriculum which the CREW method does not consider.

Case 20: Student Is Injured Moving Equipment

Description

Riley High School's media center has an active group of student assistants in the school media center. Over 50 enroll for credit each semester. The students assist in all aspects of the program. Some seniors even help teach the freshmen how to use the library, and other seniors visit elementary schools twice a week to help in those libraries. A student can earn credit not only by electing to volunteer through the media center, but by acting as a "student secretary" through the business department as long as the student meets certain requirements.

A major force behind the development of this extensive student program was the assistant media specialist, Betsy Burns. She had invested many hours in written policies and procedures to justify the program for credit.

One popular area for students, of course, is the audiovisual department. Here some students are able to do minor repairs of equipment and often demonstrate the use of new equipment to teachers. Student assistants also move equipment from one room to another during the school day. The building was constructed in the 1930s and is three stories high. Equipment often is moved from floor to floor through the use of the elevator located next to the media center. A few remote areas of the building, however, require that equipment be carried down a flight of stairs, usually about 10 steps. Videotape equipment with heavy television monitors and large 16mm projectors are often transported up and down these stairs to the vocational education wing. Student assistants are instructed to move the equipment while classes are in session, so the halls are not congested with students passing between classes. Carts with a monitor or a projector are "top-heavy." Not only is it difficult for the students to push the carts, but it is also difficult for the students to see where they are going.

Several precautions have been explained to the student assistants, in addition to moving equipment during light traffic times. Students are to pull equipment carts onto the elevator, not push them. Students are not to race carts down the hall or attempt to ride on them. And whenever the video equipment or a large projector has to be moved, two assistants are to be responsible, one to guide and the other to provide the "power" to move the cart.

With such an active program, however, accidents can happen. Jimmy Daniels, a new student assistant, took it upon himself to move some video equipment to the vocational wing. The cart with the monitor fell down the stairs. Jimmy was scraped by the falling television and cut by some of the shattering glass. Five stitches were needed. Jimmy's parents scheduled a meeting with the principal to discuss "safety in the media center."

As the school media specialist, consider:

a. What are the potential dangers in operating the equipment as well as in moving it?
b. What precautions can be taken to reduce the possibility of accidents?
c. What will your approach be to meeting in the principal's office with Jimmy's parents?

Response

THERE IS DANGER

What are the potential dangers in operating the equipment as well as in moving of it?

Potential dangers include:

1. Carts that are top-heavy. Injuries and even deaths have resulted when carts are tipped over and the equipment has fallen on the student. Televisions and 16mm projectors fall under this category.
2. Hot lamps being replaced in projectors, resulting in the student being burned.
3. Revolving reels on 16mm projectors, causing cuts and possible broken bones.
4. Overhead projectors that do not have the lens arm securely attached to the platform. These may fall and glass may shatter.
5. Failure to unplug equipment before changing lamps or doing other minor repair work. This can cause electrocution.

6. Lamps that are broken in the process of removal from a projector, causing cuts.
7. Use of a laminating press or tacking iron, equipment that is very hot and can burn someone.
8. Carts that are not well-constructed and that come apart, causing equipment to fall.
9. Removal of the safety or ground wire from the electrical socket, which can result in electrocution.

What precautions can be taken to reduce the possibility of accidents?

1. Don't let students work with the equipment. This especially applies to elementary students. They may not have the physical development necessary to handle certain situations.
2. Send more than two students when moving large equipment. In this situation it should be made clear that television monitors should be taken off the cart before the cart is moved down the stairs. More student or teacher help would facilitate this.
3. Hold safety workshops with the students. Require them to pass a safety test before they are allowed to have any contact with audiovisual equipment.
4. Require the students *and parents* to sign a contract stating that they understand the dangers involved in working with audiovisual equipment before the students can work in the department.
5. Determine whether your school has a written policy statement involving school safety standards. If not, work on one. *(DPD)*

LEGAL QUESTIONS

On the legal questions concerning who is to blame, you need to look to state statutes, which may require that certain questions be raised. Was the school exercising "reasonable care"? Did the injury result from the act or omission by the media specialist in performing her job? Was the risk involved both foreseeable and unreasonable? Would such an act have been avoided by the reasonably prudent person? Thus the whole idea of what constitutes *reasonable* must be judged by the courts, taking into consideration the parties involved, the degree of danger present, the conduct of the parties, the issue of foreseeability, and the level of care or precaution taken by the supervisor. *(LYF)*

DON'T EXPECT STUDENTS TO DO MORE THAN THEY ARE ABLE

Students should never be asked or expected to carry heavy equipment or to move equipment that is larger than themselves! These jobs should be left to adult custodial personnel.

1. Permanently assign one of each type of equipment (i.e., one 16mm projector, one VCR, etc.) to each area of the building that is accessible only by use of stairs.
2. If not enough equipment is available, teachers will need to bring their classes to a room in a more accessible part of the building when they need to use heavy AV equipment. A strong effort should be made to obtain enough funds to purchase equipment that can be permanently assigned to these inaccessible areas so that equipment can be more conveniently located. The incident such as the one discussed should more than adequately prove the need for such additional equipment!
3. Attach safety signs to each cart.
4. No carts should be used that are higher than 42 inches. *(JJ)*

BIBLIOGRAPHY

Delisle, James R. "Saying 'No' for Safety's Sake." *Ohio Media Spectrum* 37(2) (1985): 57–60.
Reactions to true stories involving elementary school students who died in accidents resulting from moving television carts.

Sorensen, Edwin. "Follow This Advice, and Make Your Schools Safer for Teachers and Kids." *American School Board Journal* 172(6) (1985): 33–34.
Sorensen explains that safety in schools has not been emphasized adequately and there is a need for better policies and more safety inspections.

Case 21: Closing the Library for Special Programs

Description

Each year many students at William Taft High School decide to do a report on the topic "Teenage Suicide." Although the school has not suffered the loss of any students in recent times from suicides, two cases of teenage suicide have taken place at the high school on the other side of town.

James Taylor, library media specialist for the high school, and Ann Kotler, director of counseling, have discussed several times the need for more information concerning this important topic. Mr. Taylor has gathered extensive information, including a resource file with newspaper clippings concerning teenage suicide. Local, experts on the topic have been guest speakers at the school. Mr. Taylor and Ms. Kotler, however, want to establish a forum in which the students who are interested and want to take part can examine the topic for a full day. This full-day activity would include films, speakers, and discussions led by the counseling staff and other experts on the topic. Students who want to attend would be required to receive permission from each of their classroom teachers. Students from the other high school would also be invited.

As the proposal is discussed with the principal, most of the necessary requirements for the seminar are approved, except for the direct involvement of the library media specialist. The proposal includes use of the school media center for the all-day event. The media center has space for both large-group presentations and small-group discussions, as well as areas in which materials can be displayed for students to borrow after the forum. Mr. Taylor wants to be involved in the activities as a resource advisor and as one who takes part in the discussions. The principal argues that this would prevent other students from using the library and would prevent teachers from using the library as well. Mr. Taylor argues that "closing the library for this one day will make more students and teachers aware of the issues, and they can make plans to be without library services for one day if the closing is announced several weeks ahead of time." Consider the following:

a. Just how active should the librarian's role be in addressing current issues that affect the students? Is Mr. Taylor moving into an area that should be left to other "experts"?
b. Are there any activities for which the library should be reserved for exclusive use?
c. Is the school library the proper place for a "public forum" on controversial issues?

Response

HAPPENINGS IN THE MEDIA CENTER

Major news events, important current social issues, and local personalities of interest often are not included in the standard curriculum of the public school. Just as the school library media center's collection of materials meets the need of providing students with access to information on subjects that are important but not given much space in the textbook nor time in class discussion, so too the library media center can provide a location for a forum to discuss the issues related to a major topic of interest. Planning the process of developing special happenings, identification of possible speakers, arranging for special films, and scheduling the event for a large portion of the school day are reasonable functions of the professional school library media specialist.

The content of special "happenings" in the school library media center can include a variety of possibilities. Some school librarians have sponsored a "Week of the Arts" with each day devoted to a different art such as "sculpture," "weaving," "glass blowing," "quilting," and "silk screening." Displays of items and related books are established not only in the library but also in other rooms of the school. Parents may be invited to attend either during the day or during an evening open-house. Student-produced items are placed on display along with examples of local artists and reproductions of classic works.

Other typical happenings or events include:

Career Day—Local citizens are invited to be available in the school library media center to discuss their chosen vocation.
International Day—Various ethnic groups will display unique dress, food, and other items that represent their special heritage.

Pet Day—Students can bring pets; displays help to promote proper care of domesticated animals.

Depending on the school's facility, it may be easier to manage such events in the school's gym or auditorium. However, the school library media center should not be ruled out as a space for such activities. Space will be needed for small group discussions, showing of films or video programs, and individual learning centers.

Such happenings create a chance to show, on a very concrete basis, the tie between information resources and current events. Most important, it is an opportunity for the school library media specialist to demonstrate that the process of interviewing fellow human beings is a major way of gaining information. Interview and listening skills can be tested through such events if teachers work with the library media center staff and develop activities through the classroom related to the event. *(DC)*

ADVOCATE DISCUSSION OF CONTROVERSIAL TOPICS

The opportunity to give attention to controversial topics should be welcomed by the skilled library media center manager. What better method to give emphasis to important topics such as "AIDS," "child abuse," and "teenage suicide?" Planned in cooperation with the administration, the school counselors, selected teachers, and community members, such events can give the emphasis to these topics that cannot be achieved through the regular classroom experience. Closing the library for the event helps to add to the importance of the happening. School library media specialists are certainly qualified to coordinate and facilitate such happening on almost any subject area, just as they have skills that allow them to deal with multidisciplines in the selection of print and nonprint materials. *(DC)*

BIBLIOGRAPHY

American Association of School Librarians and Association for Educational Communications and Technology. *Information Power: Guidelines for School Library Media Programs.* Chicago: American Library Association, 1988.
See pages 14–21. "The center itself attracts students and is organized so that many activities can occur simultaneously."

American Library Association Task Force on Excellence in Education. *Realities: Educational Reform in a Learning Society.* Chicago: American Library Association, 1985.
This pamphlet provides a philosophy for dealing with lifelong learning skills and involving the school and public library in current social issues as well as the traditional support for a literate society.

Kimzey, Ann C., Patricia Wilson, and Linda Garner. "School Library Programming with Community Resources." *Top of the News* 41(1) (1984): 89–92.
Suggests utilizing community resources for school library programming. Topics include establishing resource files, preparation and objectives of the program, coordinating publicity, and documentation of the program.

Phi Delta Kappan 70(4) (1988): 290–98.
Three important articles are provided in this issue that suggest information and materials of use in special programs on teenage suicide: "Understanding and Preventing Teen Suicide: An Interview with Barry Garfinkel," "Adolescent Suicide—An Open Letter to Counselors," and "Providing Reasons for Wanting to Live."

Reed, Sally. "KAPPAN Special Report — Children with AIDS: How Schools Are Handling the Crisis." *Phi Delta Kappan* 69(5) (1988): K1–12.
This is a valuable guide to issues and resources for the school media specialist who wants to work with others in the school and community to make critical information available.

Waters, Kate. "Boston Public Presents Forum on Teen Suicide." *American Libraries* 16(3) (1985): 184–85.
A large public library establishes a forum on a current critical issue. Could the school library do the same? (As this case was being written, the United States Supreme Court was handing down a decision concerning student newspaper coverage of issues such as teen suicide, abortion, and AIDS. The Court found that the administration did have the power to limit such publications, and the arguments from this and other related cases may prove to be of interest to the question of special forums which might be held in the school library.)

Wilson, Evie. "The Librarian as Advocate for Youth." In *Reaching Young People through Media.* Edited by Nancy Bach Pillon, pp. 155–80. Littleton, CO: Libraries Unlimited, 1983.
"A youth advocate is a person who believes in creating the conditions under which young people may make their own decisions affecting their own lives." Wilson gives a very complete review of how the librarian establishes such a role.

Wilson, Patricia J., and Ann C. Kimzey. *Happenings: Developing Successful Programs for School Libraries.* Littleton, CO: Libraries Unlimited, 1987.
Provides examples of "traditional" events that can bring excitement to the school library environment. Most examples deal with elementary and junior high schools, although senior high school events are mentioned. Of specific use will be the suggestions about how to evaluate such happenings with feedback from teachers and students. One chapter provides excellent ideas on how to develop a community resource file.

Case 22: Purchase without Preview

Description

The microcomputer revolution has hit Elmwood Junior High School. A fund is available for teachers to purchase software. Each department has been granted funding to spend on software over the school year, and indications are that the funding will increase even more in the coming years. The school board wants this school district to be "the leader in the use of modern technology to teach young people."

With many departmental budgets being increased threefold, the teachers have been seeking flyers, computer magazine ads, and software reviews in order to make "wise" purchases. Funding given specifically for computer software has increased in the library budget as well.

Elmwood Junior High School has a student enrollment of 900 and a teacher staff of 55. Classes are small, and the school has always had a great deal of support for purchase of instructional materials.

Neil Barns, the school librarian and media specialist, has been able to involve teachers in the selection process before. Each department holds an annual meeting with the librarian to identify specific material needs. This year, however, departments have decided to experiment with their additional funding, and teachers have been allotted individual amounts to order "any software they feel is worthwhile." By the end of the year, the teachers discover that many of the programs are not "as advertised" and much of the software will not be of value in the classroom.

As Mr. Barns, consider:

a. Why is there a need for the media specialist to play a role in coordinating departmental materials funding with that of the media center?

b. Should you suggest an approach for coordinating the review, selection, and acquisition of software? What is the role of the school library media specialist?

c. What issues must be addressed when departments build their own collection of instructional materials (materials which will not be shared with other departments)?

Response

MEDIA SPECIALIST AS COORDINATOR

No department head wants to waste money on the purchase of learning resources, especially on items that will never be used. In selecting resources, it is vital for teachers to recognize the special expertise of the building's library media specialist. He or she is cognizant of the curriculum, of the present collection, and of the reviewing sources. It would be foolish not to cooperate with this person.

The principal must take the lead and demand adherence to the same efficient practices in the preview and selection of computer software as for all other materials. Does the district have a selection policy that addresses the need for preview of expensive, innovative or potentially controversial materials?

The school library media specialist is the resource expert on the faculty who can coordinate all discipline areas, reading interests, and reading abilities. Even when a specific department makes final decisions on the purchase of materials, the media specialist is still the professional who can expedite the acquisition of the materials through the best jobber, and can often prevent expensive duplication of effort and duplication of materials purchased. In addition, the school library media specialist is the resident expert of resource sharing. As school library networks grow, there will be an increase in the number of occasions when necessary materials can be borrowed from other schools or from community libraries. Development of computerized union catalogs, of course, helps to enhance this networking effort. *(JM)*

STUDENT FIELD TESTING

It has been documented that computer software producers seldom field test materials before they are placed on the market. Such materials, unlike films and videotape programs, can be revised *as teachers purchase and use the materials in the classroom.* Although such field testing may lead to a more effective instructional product eventually, those who have first invested in the program may find that there are serious problems. A practice that should be adopted by schools is to secure an agreement with the producer that with the purchase of the current program, future revised programs will be made available either free of charge or at a minimal cost.

Most distributors of software allow a 30-day preview of microcomputer software. Selection policies should strongly discourage any staff member from copying the programs during this interval. The preview period is essential for selection of most microcomputer software because:

a. Microcomputer software is expensive.
b. Such software is often so individualized that a brief written review of the product from a selection source will not cover the full potential or lack of potential.
c. It permits time for students as well as teachers to examine the programs and to see how the programs accommodate an individualized approach and various user ability level.
d. There is a great deal of duplication of programs as far as their intended objectives, but only a few quality programs which will truly meet the instructional need.

Coordination of the field testing of the software with teachers and students being active in the process can become an excellent opportunity for the library media specialist to take command of the selection process. Many models for evaluation forms exist in the literature. Written evaluations often generate a record that allows schools in the same area to share opinions and judgments. Some schools have become part of a regional computer evaluation network that sponsors computer software media fairs several times a year. Teachers and media specialists gather for an afternoon and evaluate new programs and exchange ideas at such fairs. *(DC)*

BIBLIOGRAPHY

American Association of School Librarians and Association for Educational Communications and Technology. *Information Power: Guidelines for School Library Media Programs.* Chicago: American Library Association, 1988.
See pages 70–75. "All formats of information are considered for the collection and are evaluated on the basis of their utility in meeting instructional, informational, and other user needs in the school community."

Callison, Daniel. "Experience and Time Investment Factors in Public School Teacher Evaluation of Educational Microcomputer Software." *Journal of Educational Technology Systems* 16(2) (1987–88): 129–50.
Evidence gathered in this project emphasized the importance of prior experience with similar educational software before a teacher makes a judgment on selection of new software programming, and the importance

of allowing enough time for the teacher to make a complete evaluation of the software.

————. "Judgment Criteria and Overall Ratings of Educational Microcomputer Software Compared Between Teacher and Student Evaluators." *Computers in the Schools* 6(2) (1989).

Results of the analysis of evaluations completed by student and teacher groups indicated that teachers tended to favor educational software that supports their current lesson plans and were designed in tutorial format. Students tended to favor simulations or problem-solving programs. Both groups tended to favor the game format least.

Callison, Daniel, and Gloria Haycock. "A Methodology for Student Evaluation of Educational Microcomputer Software." *Educational Technology* 28(1) (1988): 25–32.

Presents a field-tested method for involving students in the evaluation of microcomputer software programs. Students in K–12 demonstrated the ability to pass judgment on the merits of various instructional formats including tutorials and simulations.

Clyde, Laurel A., and Joan D. Joyce. "Selecting Computer Software for School Libraries." *School Library Media Quarterly* 13(2) (1985): 129–37.

The authors examine criteria for software selection and the use of software packages in school library management. Review sources are also mentioned.

Evaluator's Guide for Microcomputer-Based Instructional Packages. Eugene, OR: International Council for Computers in Education, 1982.

This selection approach developed by MicroSIFT, a project of the Computer Technology Program at the Northwest Regional Educational Laboratory, is clear and well defined. A standard selection form is enclosed in the guide, and all important criteria are explained. Sample evaluations are also included.

Haycock, Gloria, and Daniel Callison. "The Need for Centralizing Control of Selection, Evaluation, and Acquisition of Microcomputer Software." *American Secondary Education* 13(2) (1984): 10–14.

Development of a "core group" is recommended so that a systematic selection process can take place. More than just preview of software, actual in-classroom field testing should take place.

Komoski, Kenneth. "Push Ed Software out of the Comfort Zone." *School Library Journal* 31(3): 56–59.

Komoski, executive director of Educational Products Information Exchange Institute, summarizes the software evaluation effort of the EPIE teams, "...they found that only about one out of four of these products [educational microcomputer software] met minimum standards of educational quality; fewer than five out of 100 were exemplary."

Lathrop, Ann, Ed. *Educational Software Preview Guide.* California TECC Software Clearinghouse, 1985– .

Contact the Professional Library and Microcomputer Center at San Mateo County Office of Education, 333 Main Street, Redwood City, CA

94063, to get on a mailing list for useful materials in the selection of microcomputer software. This guide allows for identification of the few programs which are worth your time and effort to request for preview by teachers and students.

Lathrop, Ann, and Bobby Goodson. *Courseware in the Classroom: Selecting, Organizing, and Using Educational Software.* Reading, MA: Addison-Wesley, 1983.
Methods for introducing computer software to the faculty are discussed. The basic principles established in this book hold true today. Lathrop is an important name to remember and trace through the literature for more information on computer software in the public schools. She edits the useful selection guide *Digest of Software Reviews.*

Troutner, Joanne. *The Media Specialist, the Microcomputer, and the Curriculum.* Edited by Shirley Aaron. Littleton, CO: Libraries Unlimited, 1983.
This was one of the first really useful tools for the school library media specialist for both selecting software and introducing computers into the school curriculum. Troutner's name is important to remember, as she reviews software on a regular basis in many publications, including *School Library Media Quarterly.*

Truett, Carol, and Lori Gillespie. *Choosing Educational Software: A Buyer's Guide.* Littleton, CO: Libraries Unlimited, 1984.
This guide deals with many selection issues, including the practice of field testing materials with students. Truett also edits a useful column, "The Computing Librarian" in the journal *The Computing Teacher.*

Case 23: The Librarian as Censor

Description

Before she stopped working to raise two sons, Amanda Bennett had been a library media specialist for 7 years in high school and middle school. She also worked part time in the children's department of the public library where her experience with children's literature was much appreciated. Ms. Bennett read constantly and kept up with trends in materials for children and young adults. She had loved doing book talks and now read to her boys at home. Her friends asked her for advice when buying books for their children and grandchildren. Ms. Bennett is a school volunteer and is interested in the library media program as a former practitioner.

One of the projects Ms. Bennett has initiated is a book discussion group at her eldest son's school. Each year the parents involved select 6 books and buy a set of 10 each to be kept in the library for the discussion group to read. The books are also available to other parents. This year, Allenton Elementary has a new library media specialist. Janice Farr is fresh out of graduate school. Maggie Peltz, one of the members of the discussion group, had been to the school to welcome Ms. Farr and to make plans for the coming year's book discussion group.

She called Ms. Bennett the evening of her visit, very upset. "Ms. Farr has rejected one of the books on our discussion group reading list," Ms. Peltz said. "We've ordered the books; what should we do?"

Ms. Bennett, who understood that the new librarian might be a little defensive or nervous during the first few months on the job, offered to talk with Ms. Farr. "Perhaps she doesn't know how our selection process works," she told Ms. Peltz.

The "talk" with Ms. Farr was unpleasant. Although the book in question had received excellent reviews in the leading selection sources and had been read by many of the mothers in the discussion group, Ms. Farr was adamant about excluding this book, not only from the list but from the collection in general. The book had the words "hell" and "jackass" in the text and a scene Ms. Farr felt was "lusty." Ms. Bennett told Ms. Farr of the reviews and the selection process and mentioned she felt the words were mild compared with what is "said in the halls." Ms. Bennett noted that other titles in the collection contained similar words as well. Ms. Farr replied, "Oh yes, I've noticed and I'm going to see that all these questionable books are discarded. We don't need books by Judy Blume or any other author who doesn't uphold traditional American values and respect for parents."

Ms. Bennett was shocked. She left the library without another word. "What can I do?" she asked herself later. "This librarian is going to strip the collection of books that most of our group feel are worth having, and parents won't even realize what is happening."

Discuss the following:

a. What is the role of parents in the selection process for materials housed in the school library?

b. What are the pressures that cause school librarians, teachers, and administrators to censor materials? What can be done to promote intellectual freedom, even on the elementary school level?

c. School selection policies are often designed to defend what is placed on the shelf. What elements of a policy should be present in order for teachers, parents, and students to question what is *not* available in the library?

Response

THE FRONTLINE CENSOR

The pressures on the school library media specialist are often great when it comes to selecting materials that "may cause controversy" in the community. On the one hand, the school librarian is expected to serve as a catalyst for new ideas and different options, as well as an advocate for the discussion of all sides of an issue. On the other hand, selecting materials that are "safe" and free of controversy will often prevent difficult-to-handle discussions and remove the librarian from the "uncomfortable" task of trying to justify some of the expenditures of the taxpayer's money. However, if the school library media specialist cannot deal with controversy and wants to live in a worry-free environment without expression of opinions that may disrupt order, why is he or she part of a profession that is founded on the principles of open and free access to all information by all people?

A librarian may have an unfounded perception of the restricting forces in the local community and, as a result, censor materials simply by not purchasing them or promoting them. In such cases, the librarian is simply using what he or she assumes to be a restrictive presence in the community to justify his or her own bias. Professional librarians who clearly and openly practice the restriction of access to materials for the purpose of censoring such information should seriously consider leaving the field. *(DC)*

WELCOME PARENT INVOLVEMENT

It is always wise to include parents on your media center committees. Parental involvement is the key to community support, especially in a censorship issue. Parents will come to the defense of the librarian (if they have been a part of the educational process) more often than they will move to censor materials. In some cases, community standards may be more conservative than those of the school personnel. In this case, the media specialist is more restrictive than the general standards of the community, and the parents have a right to be concerned.

Ms. Bennett should go to the principal and the district media director, if there is one, and express her concern. Censorship is even more insidious when materials are not purchased or are removed by the professional. These books have passed the school's criteria for selection; therefore, the principal should question Ms. Farr's authority to remove the materials without any proper review. *(JM)*

BIBLIOGRAPHY

American Association of School Librarians and Association for Educational Communications and Technology. *Information Power: Guidelines for School Library Media Programs.* Chicago: American Library Association, 1988.
See pages 5–7, 140–48. "Library media specialists are dedicated to providing access to information and ideas for all those served by the library media program."

Bauer, Marion Dane. "The Censor Within." *Top of the News* 41(1) (1984): 67–71.
A librarian reviews the experiences she has had with censorship and gives some insight into the school librarian's role in defending intellectual freedom.

Censorship or Selection: Choosing Books for Public Schools. New York: Media and Society Seminars, 1982. 60-minute videocassette.
Kurt Vonnegut, Judy Blume, Moral Majority activist Ronald S. Godwin, and various educators and parents participate in a seminar conducted to discuss the issue of censorship in school libraries and the classroom. The resulting confrontation evokes not only sharp differences of opinion, but surprising areas of agreement.

Davis, James E. *Dealing with Censorship.* Urbana, IL: National Council of Teachers of English, 1979.
A collection of essays which have much to say to educators concerning censorship issues in the schools. Gives special attention to Edward B. Jenkinson, Kenneth L. Donelson, and Allan Glatthorn.

Donelson, Ken. "Six Statements/Questions from the Censors." *Phi Delta Kappan* 69(3) (1987): 208–14.
A discussion of recent issues related to censorship of materials in public schools, including secular humanism. Donelson gives attention to reported censorship practiced by teachers and librarians.

Farmer, Rod. "Toward a Definition of Secular Humanism." *Contemporary Education* 58(3) (1987): 126–30.
Farmer refutes arguments that secular humanism is a religion.

Fiske, Marjorie. *Book Selection and Censorship.* Berkeley, CA: University of California Press, 1968.
This is a classic study often cited in the literature as one which has established the foundation for more recent inquiries concerning censorship pressures in the public schools and the reactions of the school librarian. Fiske concentrated on the California schools.

Jenkinson, Edward B. *Censors in the Classroom.* Carbondale, IL: Southern Illinois University Press, 1979.
This publication is subtitled "The Mind Benders" and Jenkinson never makes any secret about who is doing the "twisting of the mind." He documents the "attacks" on educational materials for various areas of the country and concentrates on "problems" in textbooks which relate to the issue of secular humanism.

——. *The Schoolbook Protest Movement.* Bloomington, IN: Phi Delta Kappan, 1986.
Jenkinson updates his 1979 publication.

Jones, Frances M. *Defusing Censorship: The Librarian's Guide to Handling Censorship Conflicts.* Phoenix, AZ: Oryx, 1983.
Chapter 10, "Internal Censorship: Putting Principles into Practice," is of specific interest for this case. Jones discusses several types of preselection censorship as well as ways librarians may tend to restrict access to some materials after they are acquired.

Office of Intellectual Freedom of the American Library Association. *Intellectual Freedom Manual.* Chicago: American Library Association, 1983.
This is the handbook of policies from the American Library Association. Contents of this publication are "must reading" for any practicing school library media specialist. A third edition of this manual is scheduled to be published before 1990.

Pierard, Richard V. "The New Religious Right and Censorship." *Contemporary Education* 58(3) (1987): 131–37.
Describes the influence of the "new religious right" on censorship in the public schools.

Serebnick, Judith. "A Review of Research Related to Censorship in Libraries." *Library Research* 1(2) (1979): 95–118.
A comprehensive review of the research related to censorship issues through the 1970s. Of interest is the discussion of the major events or "variables" which seem to have an influence on the actions of the librarian as he or she makes decisions in selection of materials and in possible defense of controversial materials.

Watson, Jerry J., and Bill C. Snider. "Book Selection Pressure on School Library Media Specialists and Teachers." *School Library Media Quarterly* 9(2) (1981): 95–101.
The results of this study reinforce the need for book selectors to read more than one selection aid when choosing books. Implications from this study clearly show that book selectors avoid selecting children's books containing objectionable content as identified by someone else.

Woods, L. B., and Lucy Salvatore. "Self-Censorship in Collection Development by High School Library Media Specialists." *School Library Media Quarterly* 9(2) (1981): 102–08.
Librarians do seem, in their selection, to be avoiding those titles that are most controversial. In other words, self-censorship does seem to be practiced by high school librarians. The presence of large numbers of materials on some sort of restricted access further indicates the reluctance of many librarians to face censorship battles.

Case 24: Computerized Overdues

Description

The Vernon High School media center is in the computer age. The media center staff has supported computer-assisted instruction and even has a special computer lab adjacent to the media center. An automated circulation system has been in place for the past 3 years, and there is more and more talk about converting the card catalog to a system that will combine the district's holdings with those of the local public library and local junior college.

Of course, overdue notices have been printed out faster and more efficiently since the computer arrived. At first, a list of all of the overdue materials was sent to each homeroom teacher, and the teachers were expected to notify each student in that homeroom of materials that needed to be returned. The new approach worked fine at first until more and more teachers failed to enforce the list. "Here it is, Monday's overdue list again." So last year the practice of sending personal notices to each student who had materials overdue was begun. These are sent to homerooms; in addition, a weekly list of late materials is posted. Finally, if the material is over 6 weeks delinquent, the computer writes a letter to the parent of the student.

No fines are charged for late return of materials; however, students are held responsible for materials lost or not returned at all. Full replacement cost is recorded and grade cards are withheld each semester until full payment is made. Seniors face not having a transcript sent to a college or potential employer until costs for lost books are settled.

The media program has grown over the past 3 years. It is a very busy place with an average of two classes in the library each period. The number of teachers assigning research projects has doubled during this time. Often students find that books and periodicals needed for assignments are missing, without a record of being checked out. Inventory last summer revealed the greatest number of missing materials in the school's history.

"We seem to get the materials back for which we have a record," stated the media specialist to the principal, "but we are losing several hundred titles each semester. These are high-demand materials. Everyone wants them for the projects being assigned and the required reports."

The head media specialist, the district media supervisor, and the school principal all agree they do not want an electronic security system. It sets an unfriendly barrier, they feel, at the circulation desk. "Kids will find a way around it," the principal reasoned.

Consider the following as the head media specialist:

a. Other approaches to remind students of overdues
b. The legality of withholding grades and transcripts
c. The trade-offs for not charging fines
d. The advantages and disadvantages of placing materials on reserve in a high school library.
e. The advantages and disadvantages of an electronic security system

Response

REWARD, DON'T PUNISH

School librarians often struggle with making the collection as open and accessible as possible to all persons, especially the students. Accepting responsibility for returning materials becomes a learning experience in the school library environment, and students should be given the opportunity to demonstrate such ability. The approach, however, should reward responsible actions rather than punish unacceptable behavior. Rewarding can be more time consuming for the librarian and there are always dangers of reward systems becoming inconsistent. Students should be encouraged to check out materials as soon as they make a choice so they don't forget and leave the library without the loan being recorded. Shortly before the end of each class period, students should be reminded to check out their materials if they have not already done so. Overdue materials should be immediately brought to the attention of the students and parents. Reminders such as "Another student is waiting to use this book," or "We will be happy to renew the book, if necessary" are common examples of positive communication.

In secondary schools, time set aside to clean out lockers will lead to many materials being returned. The school library may want to "sponsor" such a locker cleaning once each semester. Student volunteers could move through the halls with carts so students can easily place materials on the carts and thus return materials to the library. The building maintenance staff will need to be a part of locker clean-out as well and they will need to place large wastebaskets in the halls. The maintenance staff can help by checking the baskets for discarded library materials which should have been returned to the media center. *(DC)*

CHECK THE LAWS

It is wise to check the laws in your own state to determine the legalities of withholding grades and transcripts. It is not legal in Indiana, for example, to withhold grades. However, a student's diploma can be withheld if he or she still owes fines or fees to the school. Thus, a record of materials not returned to the library may lead to a fine or a demand that the student (or the parents) pay for lost materials. Such a process must include documentation showing that the student had been informed of such possible charges in advance of the graduation exercises. A record of correspondence to the student, including reminders about late materials and the market value of the materials that were not returned might be held in either the library or the main office.

Charging fines is archaic and doesn't really help get materials returned to libraries. The time spent on collecting fines is not cost effective. A computer system that will flag a student's record when he or she is at the circulation desk and a method for then immediately calling overdue materials to the attention of the student would probably work better than a fine system. *(JM)*

RESERVE SHELVING

One method of saving high-demand items for student assignments is to put them on reserve. This may create a barrier to some degree, but in reality, it allows a broader access to the high-demand materials. One of our local high schools has a reputation for establishing a large reserve section with an adult volunteer or clerk to supervise the circulation of the materials. Books for assignments are kept there as well as the popular items that have high potential for being stolen. A reserve collection is a reasonable solution to a difficult question. The media specialist might also enlist the student council's help and publicize the reserve system and the reason it has been established.

One abuse of the reserve shelf that takes place in public school libraries is the placing of controversial materials "on reserve" and thus creating an unfounded barrier to the access of such information. In some cases, duplicate copies of the very popular and/or highly controversial materials should be purchased. One copy can then be placed on reserve for establishing "sure" access to those who ask, and additional copies can be placed in the general collection with open access for those who seek such information on their own. *(DC)*

EXPENSE OF ELECTRONIC SECURITY

The expense of an electronic security system must be measured against the expense of replacing materials lost through theft. Most high school librarians who have security systems feel that such systems "pay for themselves within just a few years." Middle and elementary schools don't have the same problems with deliberate theft as might be found in high schools, so such systems are probably not economically feasible at the lower grade levels. In some library environments, electronic security systems have created a barrier to students using the library, and the system itself becomes something "to beat" or "get around." Such game-playing often disappears when students begin to understand that the system is in place to help them have access to materials that others may borrow. The alarm should never result in a "major incident" that draws the attention some students are seeking. *(DC)*

BIBLIOGRAPHY

Bates, Wilma H. "Managing Overdues in the School Library." *Library and Archival Security.* 6(2/3) (1984): 83–90.
This article examines the overdues procedures of a high school library in which the librarian used a microcomputer to assist in the process. School system regulations and library policies are outlined. Through automatic sorting and updating of files, the time required to maintain overdue files was cut in half.

Sussman, Valerie. "Computerizing an Elementary School Library—A First Experience." *Catholic Library World* 58(3) (1986): 126–28.
This article describes the first attempt to automate an intermediate school library. The first priority for this library was to computerize the circulation system. Advantages and disadvantages are discussed.

Truett, Carol. "To Fine or Not to Fine: One School Library's Experience." *Top of the News* 37(3) (1981): 277–80.
Describes the experience of a middle school library which instituted a no-fines policy and summarizes the benefits of such a policy with regard to book losses and public relations.

Woolls, Blanche. "The Use of Technology in the Administration Function of School Library Media Programs." 1982. ERIC document ED 225 553.
This report gives some conclusions of a study of current use of microcomputer technology in the administration of school libraries. Scheduling, circulation, and security systems are discussed.

Case 25: Memorial Book Collection

Description

A former chairperson of the high school's English department has died at the age of 80. This teacher had been a respected and loved member of the high school faculty and the community during 40 years of teaching service. Over those years, this teacher directed several hundred dramatic productions and all-school musicals. Hundreds of graduates remember this teacher as being a "guiding force" in their lives and "an inspiration to life-long learning."

A memorial fund has been established, and contributions will be gathered for the purpose of providing materials to the school that will honor the memory of this teacher. The committee responsible for the fund has decided to use part of the money to finance remodeling of the drama department's costume, props, and makeup rooms. The board of education is delighted. The committee requests that a portion of the funds also be spent on books for the library. The committee votes unanimously to invest $3,000 in books about Shakespeare, his plays, and other classical works of English drama. These materials should be housed on special shelves, according to the committee, under a portrait of the teacher, next to the main circulation desk of the school's library.

As the school's head media specialist, how should you respond to:

    a. A committee recommending how money should be spent on materials for the library collection?

    b. A special area in the library established as a memorial to a former teacher?

Response

LISTEN AND SEEK COMPROMISE

Committees who raise money are usually in the position to say how it should be spent. If the library media specialist wants to offer an opinion, he or she should become part of the committee. In this case, take the money and buy what was requested for the theater project, unless you can prove nobody studies Shakespeare anymore.

The demand for special placement of the materials is worth an argument. The committee should be informed of the reason that materials are organized in a systematic manner for the library collection. Mention the difficulty of shelving materials out of order, unless the intent is that they never be used. Note that a precedent could be established under this practice that would lead to many, small specialized collections. Emphasize the space that this would consume and the confusion it could cause.

Offer to display a portrait of the teacher in the general area of the English literature collection. This will pay honor to the teacher and bring some attention to that area of the collection. A special display of materials that are related to the Shakespeare could be established once a year, "in memory of the teacher." Over time, such a display would probably become less and less important. *(MMJ)*

DIFFICULT TO MOVE

Two of the most difficult things to move are cemeteries and public schools. Establishing a memorial section within the school library creates a third. The collection development policy should address the establishment of memorial collections or gifts. It should state that the selection of materials is made under the guidance of the school library media specialist, and all the gifts must conform to the established selection guidelines or they are subject to being rejected for the collection. Thus, such committees should be encouraged to donate their money to the library with the understanding that the librarian, with input from teachers and students under the established selection process, will acquire the materials. It should be understood that the most reasonable approach is to acquire such materials over time, perhaps over several years, so money is not "squandered" on whatever is on the market at the time in order to expend all funds as soon as possible.

The policy should also note that establishing permanent special areas in the school library is not the best practice because of the space such collections demand. Often a school library program needs all the space necessary just to maintain its regular collection. The policy might indicate that a practical solution is to place a nameplate especially designed to honor the deceased in each book purchased from the special fund. Finally, the policy should emphasize that all of the materials purchased through the special fund are subject to the same reevaluation procedures or weeding guidelines as other books in the collection. If a book that has been purchased for this special collection becomes out-of-date, or seems to not be of use, then the librarian should retain the right to remove the material. *(DC)*

BIBLIOGRAPHY

Futas, Elizabeth, ed. *Library Acquisition Policies and Procedures.* Phoenix, AZ: Oryx Press, 1984.
This valuable guide to the development of collection policies provides several sample statements concerning gifts. See pages 444–53.

Kemp, Betty. *School Library and Media Center Acquisitions Policies and Procedures.* Phoenix, AZ: Oryx Press, 1986.
An excellent collection of model collection development policies for school libraries. Several examples of statements concerning memorial gifts will be found here.

Lane, Alfred H. *Gifts and Exchange Manual.* Westport, CT: Greenwood Press, 1980.
Although aimed at academic libraries and rare book collections, this publication gives several ideas about how memorial gifts should be handled.

Part III
Managing Facilities and Budgets to Plan for the Future

Case 26: Using Funds to Target Specific Units

Description

Over the past 5 years as the media specialist at Wilson Junior High School, Jane Summers has found there are several different responses from teachers involving the selection and use of materials. Some recommend purchase of materials and immediately work the new books or nonprint media into classroom assignments. Often these are the teachers who also help her seek out materials from other local library collections and who willingly help her evaluate the collection by helping with inventory and weeding of titles.

Other teachers seem to be eager to recommend materials for purchase, but seldom use the materials once they have been received. Often, it seems to Ms. Summers, these teachers like to spend the money but want to do little to change the way things are done in the classroom. These teachers seldom bring students to the media center or plan units of study with her. The materials recommended by these teachers seem to be quality materials, usually receiving favorable comments in the review sources.

Still other teachers refuse to recommend purchase of any materials. A few have even voiced the opinion that investment of money in media center materials takes away from the funds their department should control for textbooks and supplies. Ms. Summers feels that in some cases these less responsive teachers represent areas of the curriculum that should be represented in the collection. She orders some materials on the chance someone might use them in the future.

As the active users of the media center develop units that become rather specialized and information demanding, more and more of her budget has been invested in these areas. In some cases she has purchased three or four duplicate copies of materials on topics for which there is an extremely high demand.

For this coming school year, Ms. Summers has decided to target specific units of study that have been designed by the more active media center users and move completely away from the nonusers.

Although her budget has grown to some degree, it is not large enough to spread over the entire curriculum. She has decided to support these heavy users in order to make a strong impact on those areas of the curriculum. The other areas will simply need to be covered with the basic reference materials, and she will wait for a teacher to take a leadership role to build a collection in his or her subject area.

Ms. Summers has decided to move from an attempt to provide a collection that covers the entire school curriculum to an approach that will target and concentrate funding for more in-depth use of the collection. This targeting will also include a reduction in the money invested in leisure reading materials such as fiction and biographies. Ms. Summers feels the local public library provides much of this material and there is no need to duplicate it in her collection.

Consider these questions related to Ms. Summers' decision:

   a. As a media specialist serving the entire school, should you ignore some areas of the curriculum and concentrate on others?
   b. What are the advantages and disadvantages of Ms. Summers' plan?
   c. What cooperative efforts are needed with the public library if this plan is to succeed?
   d. What role does a collection policy play in Ms. Summers' decision?

Response

CONCENTRATE FUNDING TO CREATE AN IMPACT ON THE CURRICULUM

If Ms. Summers waits "for a teacher to take a leadership role to build a collection in his or her subject area," that collection may never be built. The bottom line for some teachers is to take the easiest route in planning their curriculum. For these teachers, often sticking to the textbook is their course of action. If Ms. Summers has decided to concentrate on materials for those teachers who have expressed the most needs, she should not announce as personal policy that she will be ignoring the remainder of the faculty. A media specialist should always keep an open ear and mind when talking with the faculty. And a media specialist must always adjust to the fact that not every teacher will utilize the media center and its materials in the same way. Teaching methods are as individual as the different teachers who make up a faculty. And different methods do not necessarily mean ineffectiveness.

It makes sense that Ms. Summers would, however, target funds for materials for those areas of the curriculum for which teachers have expressed a need. The advantages of such a situation are that library materials will be used instead of sitting on shelves and, also, student learning will be more diverse using library materials instead of just a text. The disadvantage of such a program is that some teachers might take offense at the situation and be totally turned off to library resources and services.

The fact that Ms. Summers is counting on the public library to provide recreational reading such as fiction and biographies means that she will need to discuss this with the public library staff. If the public library can meet these needs for the students, the faculty and students will need some information about this service. Ms. Summers will also need to consider whether all students in her school district have access to the public library's collection. *(MMJ)*

TARGET TO INNOVATE

Funding for school library materials is often limited and has generally declined over the past two decades compared with its "peak" in the 1960s. Part of the cause for this decline may very well be the lack of direct influence on the curriculum because of the failure to use resource materials from the library or failure to develop a collection that offers information sources to support innovative curriculum. This is stating the case in reverse from what is usually heard. Many of the most innovative and experimental instructional units will never become reality until the librarian has invested the "seed" money for the resources. Therefore, while it is true that parts of the collection will grow based on increased demand or greater circulation, other areas of the collection will need to be enhanced because the media specialist sees potential for the use of the new resources.

Often the priming or seeding of a portion of the collection will require investment in enough resource materials to meet the information needs of several students. One or two books on capital punishment or AIDS will not meet the demands of several classes assigned current affairs reports. Time and effort must also be given to building resources for a vertical file. Thus, the school library media specialist may give parent volunteers a list of specific issues or topics and ask them to search out newspaper articles on these issues or locate addresses of organizations that would supply pamphlets or magazines on the targeted subjects.

Targeting is a risk. On the one hand you can target funds to meet those areas of the curriculum that have proved to be popular and you can map the high use of such areas of the collection and build on those strengths. Those who have worked with classes know that popular topic areas require a great deal of materials, both in variety and in duplication as more than one student begins work on the same topic. On the other hand, targeting is also necessary in order to set priorities on what potential new areas of interest might be "sparked" into units of study. The risk, of course, is that the materials may not be used to the extent one originally expected. However, simply spreading the collection budget thinly over all areas will result in few if any "pockets of plenty" from which several students can draw materials, compare information, and satisfy the basic information needs of the given assignment. *(DC)*

BIBLIOGRAPHY

American Association of School Librarians and Association for Educational Communications and Technology. *Information Power: Guidelines for School Library Media Programs.* Chicago: American Library Association, 1988.
See pages 124–30. "In addition to mere numbers that would indicate the need for increased budgeting, there are other variables that will affect the budget request...."

Callison, Daniel. "Methods for Measuring Student Use of Databases and Interlibrary Loan Materials." *School Library Media Quarterly* 16(2) (1988): 138–42.
A statistical method is introduced which will assist the library media specialist in identification of "key sources" or those materials which seemed to be essential to the student in order to complete his or her paper because of the relative high number of footnotes drawn from the source.

Ho, May Lein, and David V. Loertscher. "Collection Mapping: The Research." *Drexel Library Quarterly* 21(2) (1985): 22–39.
This review has some very constructive and practical examples of collection mapping. Of specific interest is the use of the popular H. W. Wilson Catalogues as a template for collection development.

Loertscher, David V. "Collection Mapping: An Evaluation Strategy for Collection Development." *Drexel Library Quarterly* 21(2) (1985): 9–21.
Describes how to target areas of the curriculum and to graphically demonstrate emphasis areas of the collection. Use of this plan can give the librarian a clear direction in collection development.

Murry, William, Marian Messervey, Barbara Dobbs, and Susan Gough. "Collection Mapping and Collection Development." *Drexel Library Quarterly* 21(2) (1985): 40–51.
Specific examples for elementary school and secondary school library media collections are documented based on the collection mapping techniques.

Woodbury, Marda. *Selecting Materials for Instruction: Issues and Policies.* Littleton, CO: Libraries Unlimited, 1979.
Woodbury gives attention to several areas of the selection process not often discussed in detail in other literature. Participant roles for teachers, parents, and students are covered. Collections for special education and individualized learning are also examined. The first part of the book, "Overviews," is a good introduction to the key factors which should be considered in the selection process.

Case 27: Is There a Need for Statistics?

Marsha Zegler has come to Lakewood School District as Director of Media Services. Her doctorate from the university is in media management. She plans to promote the role of the media specialist in instructional design and wants the highest level of involvement advocated by leaders in the field. She hopes for each media program to have an interactive approach which integrates information skills into all areas of the curriculum.

As a beginning activity to reach this goal, Dr. Zegler has asked the 12 media specialists in each of Lakewood's 10 schools to keep detailed statistical records of the work they are doing.

Everyone has moaned and groaned about this added task, but LuAnn Williams at Oakridge Junior High is furious. Her program, in a school of 600 sixth to ninth graders, is noted for its excellence. She has only a half-time clerk and always works extra hours at school and at home. "Gathering statistics to improve a well-run, vital program is ridiculous," says Ms. Williams. "I don't have time to eat lunch most days. There is no way I can stop and write down what I'm doing. If I do, I'll have to give up some service I'm giving the kids or the teachers. I'm helping the teachers teach and students learn. Why do I have to keep statistics on it?"

Consider the following:

    a. Is there a legitimate rationale that Dr. Zegler can give Ms. Williams for gathering the statistics she feels are needed?

    b. Is there some other method of proving her program that Ms. Williams might use to show she has reached an interactive involvement in instruction?

    c. What are some of the benefits of showing the activities of a successful program to others?

Response

TO JUSTIFY THE BUDGET

It is not unrealistic for media specialists to be able to document how the media program is an integral part of the total curriculum; however, in this instance the new director, who apparently has high expectations from the media programs, may have failed in her approach with her staff. It may seem that she has little regard for what is already being done without taking time to become acquainted with the existing program.

Today's budget crunch has brought many changes in the way media programs need to be evaluated and promoted. While her approach may have been unrealistic, there is a need to be able to provide information showing how the media center program is an integral part of the curriculum if media centers are to continue to receive funding.

Media specialists do feel pressed for time, and if there is a good program in existence, it is not difficult to document these activities. The new director may need to do some inservicing to show how easy it can be to keep records of what is being accomplished within the existing program. Each time the media specialist works with a teacher to plan units, projects, and programs that work can be readily documented through the use of a simple planning sheet. This might include the name of the unit, class, class size, objectives, materials to be used, length of project, and evaluation. As these records are accumulated throughout the year one can readily gather information to provide statistics regarding the media program.

In many cases, using the technique of random sampling will not take away from time that should be spent with teachers and teaching. Perhaps these are methods which Ms. Williams could use to show how her program is involved.

Media centers need to promote their programs to keep the public informed of their activities. This information can have a large impact on future funding for materials and programs.

In addition, by publicizing ideas and activities, media specialists find they have common programs as well as problems. This interaction is healthy to the growth and development of new programs. *(GH)*

BE SELECTIVE WITH STATISTICS

Statistics mean nothing unless there are comparisons that can be made, comparisons based on the same factors. A school principal once asked me if a circulation of 5,000 books in his elementary school library was good. That would be difficult to say, unless we could compare that with circulation figures for other elementary schools of the same size, with the same circulation policy (the same rules for number of books that could be loaned and amount of time loaned) and the same offerings in the collection. If all of those factors were equal (and they never seem to be), one might be able to compare circulation figures of two elementary schools and say one school is loaning more materials per student than the other school. But even then, one cannot say which of the circulation records is "better." It may be that one school has a much lower circulation per student than a comparable school on the other side of town, but this school's book circulation has increased to nearly double what it was the year before. Maybe the school's circulation of books is not as high as others, but there are signs that progress is being made.

In order to have meaning, tabulations must be made with specific questions in mind about what one wants to know, and then data should be gathered in a systematic manner. Further, since it takes time to gather enough information for it to be meaningful, one must be ready to give time to the process so that figures can be gathered over several years. The media specialist would decide what some useful questions might be, and how useful or important the answers to those questions might be. Do you want to show that you are doing more than another school of comparable size and with comparable staffing? Do you want to show that your program is improving each year?

In addition, because the process is time-consuming, one should be selective about the specific statistics gathered. Quantitative measures can be very impressive and can serve a purpose which will lead to greater support of the program. There seems to be no standard in the school library media field that specifies what should be tabulated or how such measurements should be made. It might be good to remember that whatever figures are gathered, they should help answer the question "What are the outputs of the school library media center?" Too often the numbers called for in state reports and reflected in national guidelines tell the library media specialist what should be invested or spent and not what should be resulting from the program. Instead of numbers that tell the school board how many books the library doesn't have compared with the national norm, it may be a better service to gather figures that reflect how much the current materials are being used.

In addition to the numbers, testimony from teachers, students, and parents will often help the school board or the principal understand the value of the services and the number of times the service has been provided. Evaluation forms which encourage patrons to praise the media center as well as to offer constructive suggestions will help the library media specialist gather such qualitative statements. Notes and letters of appreciation should be sought and kept to use as documentation of the success of the program. I can remember one high school media specialist who kept attendance records from one year to the next of the special presentations of student oral histories produced through the media center. Each year the attendance went up, each year the number of student products went up, and each year there were more and more calls from the community to use the student productions at local organizations' programs. The most impressive record of this activity, however, was the scrapbook compiled each year. Letters from students, from those interviewed for the projects, and from parents who saw their children engaged in a constructive activity were gathered along with the flyers and photos used to promote the program. These statements were impressive and gave life and meaning to the numbers. *(DC)*

BIBLIOGRAPHY

American Association of School Librarians. *A Planning Guide for Information Power.* Chicago: American Library Association, 1988.
This is an easy-to-follow, clear guide to the important process of writing mission statements, goals, objectives, and plans for activities. The guide gives the correct emphasis to involvement of many individuals from teachers to parents to principals in the planning process under the leadership of the building-level school library media specialist. The guide also has an excellent chapter on "collecting needed information." The discussion in this chapter is important because of the use of such terms as "baseline date," "ratios," "logs and anecdotal records," and the argument for clear presentation of the data to groups who will have an impact on possible changes in the library media center program and budget. The only troublesome line in the guide is "Planning is critical, but it must not be done at the expense of your current program!" Such advice is very misleading. Planning is the most important fuction of the library media specialist who has a vision to justify, document, and bring to reality. Knowing that selected statistics, presented in a clear manner, will help the vision become reality is also important. Giving time to this data collection and analysis process is essential, regardless of how successful one may regard his or her current media program.

American Association of School Librarians and Association for Educational Communications and Technology. *Information Power: Guidelines for School Library Media Programs.* Chicago: American Library Association, 1988.
See pages 113–30. "Quantitative descriptions are limited in value because the quantitative characteristics of [media] programs vary in relationship to needs and program activities."

Callison, Daniel J. "Methods for Measuring Student Use of Databases and Interlibrary Loan Materials." *School Library Media Quarterly* 16(2) (1988): 138–42.
Demonstrates how to gather data on student use of materials in order to determine key sources and databases used most successfully.

————. "You, Too, Are an Important Resource." *Instructional Innovator* 25(7) (1980): 25.
This article includes a checklist of areas in instructional design for which statistics should be kept to show the extent of such services.

Daniel, Evelyn H. "Performance Measures for School Librarians: Complexities and Potential." In *Advances in Librarianship: Volume 6.* Edited by Melvin J. Voigt and Michael Harris, pp. 1–51. New York: Academic Press, 1976.
An in-depth discussion concerning some ideas on gathering meaningful statistics on school library use. This also gives a historical perspective to the use of quantitative measures in school library standards.

Loertscher, David V. *Taxonomies of the School Library Media Program.* Englewood, CO: Libraries Unlimited, 1988.
Although Loertscher has many suggestions as to how one might gather data, few specific end products are presented. His ideas, however, on data for justification in collection development and evaluation of the library media program, are always worth considering.

Mancall, Jacqueline C., and M. Carl Drott. *Measuring Student Information Use.* Littleton,CO: Libraries Unlimited, 1983.
Gives the step-by-step process for gathering data and applying analysis of what documents students use as reflected in the bibliography of the student's paper. Such data, along with the expertise of the experienced media specialist, can help to support some important changes in the development of the collection.

Miller, Inabeth. "A House of Bricks." National Center for Education Statistics, Washington, DC, 1985. ERIC document ED 272 556.
School libraries and media centers have been neglected in analyses of educational assessment and as instruments for educational improvement. Although statistics have been gathered on the number of books owned, information is also needed about the collection's currency, value, and utilization. Information should also be collected about the nonprint materials and students' use of databases and computers. As computer use increases in the school curriculum, better ways to collect data on their use are needed.

Miller, Marilyn L., and Barbara B. Moran. "Expenditures for Resources in School Library Media Centers: FY '82–'83." *School Library Journal* 30(2) (1983): 105–14; "Expenditures for Resources in School Library Media Centers: FY '85–'86." *School Library Journal* 33(10) (1987): 37–45.
From this gathering of statistics on a national scale, the school media specialist has one reference point against which local statistics can be compared.

Van House, Nancy A., et al. *Output Measures for Public Libraries.* Chicago: American Library Association, 1987.
Although designed for adult services for the public library, school library media specialists should give attention to the simple and understandable data-gathering methods outlined in this ALA publication. Together with the manual *Planning & Role Setting for Public Libraries,* some models for setting goals and measuring the effect of services to reach those goals

is nicely presented. School library media specialists should look for the future work of Douglas L. Zweizig or Eleanor Jo Rodger as they may be presenting in the future tested methods for measuring services to children and young adults. They should also check a chapter by Shirley A. Fitzgibbons titled "Accountability of Library Services for Youth: A Planning, Measurement and Evaluation Model," scheduled for publication in 1989 in the book *Measurement and Evaluation of Library Services* (Norwood, NJ: Ablex).

Case 28: Understanding the Budget

Description

Rhonda White, who has been the head media specialist for a senior high school library for 5 years, finds each year that the needs of her collection often do not match the amounts allotted in the budget of the school corporation. For example, last year she determined through her extensive selection process that over $2,000 of additional nonprint items were requested and justified by her teachers, but the amount specifically budgeted for nonprint items fell $800 short of covering those requests. The book budget, on the other hand, was more than enough to cover the titles selected. As a matter of fact, she found she had over $1,000 left in the print budget by May 1, the deadline for all funds to be exhausted, but could not use that extra money to cover the nonprint items.

When her new budget was issued in July of the current school year, Ms. White found that the budget lines had been adjusted. Her nonprint budget line was increased by the usual 3%, or about $60. Her book budget line, however, had been reduced by $1,000. When she investigated the change, she was informed that since she did not spend the entire print budget the previous year, her needs did not justify the additional $1,000 for books.

When Ms. White argued that the budget does not allow her to shift funding to cover the materials needed by the teachers from one given year to the next, she was informed that such budget lines are determined and defined by the state. Budget lines for "Print Materials," "Nonprint Materials," "Microcomputer Software," "Equipment," and "Materials and Supplies" define the areas in which funds can be provided.

Consider the following:

a. How can Ms. White plan ahead in order to work within the restrictions of the current budget outline?

b. What alternative budget approaches should Ms. White consider?

  c. What external funds are possible for Ms. White to acquire in order for her to meet some needs that are beyond her given budget?

  d. In what ways can Ms. White provide evidence that will change and adjust her budget for the coming year?

  e. In reality, do state guidelines on school budgeting actually create unmanageable restrictions for local programs?

Response

STATE GUIDELINES ARE A FRAMEWORK

The case of "understanding the budget" is not as unusual as it appears on the surface. The problem is not one of state budgetary restrictions, but rather, one of planning and communication on the part of the media specialist.

My personal approach to this problem may require 2 years of work to be successful. Completing these simple tasks may be helpful.

1. If the funding is there, *spend it!*
2. Be polite and calm with your school treasurer.
3. Have the treasurer explain each of the accounts you are responsible for, the items that may be purchased through them, and the time frame in which the money must be spent.
4. Know *when* the budget allocations are made for the coming school year.
5. Proceed with your usual staff surveys and needs assessments before the first semester is completed. Save all of these records.
6. Keep a "wish list," and note how much those items will cost.
7. Meet with your principal, treasurer, or superintendent before allocations are made. Express your thoughts on how much money should be in each account. At this time, present your documentation for your requests and the *reasons why a better education will be provided to all students.*
8. Always leave a small amount of funds to cover emergencies, out of stocks, or errors.

State budget guidelines are intended to provide a framework for how funds can be expended. The distribution of local funds into those accounts can and should be determined with the input of the building expert—the media specialist. *(JAB)*

RANK REQUESTS

Ms. White needs to know more about the budget-making process. Since she must live with the budget as it was written for this school year, she should examine the needs and requests of faculty members, asking that they rank requests. She could also attempt to have the amounts within the library budget line items adjusted by presenting a rationale for such shifts to her administrators.

She should have a file of backup requests for purchase and/or a file of additions to the collection that have been preselected by her so that funds in her budget never go unspent.

Ms. White could also investigate the possibility of outside sources of funds. These possibilities could include grants from government or private organizations such as parent-teacher associations, memorial foundations, clubs, and business and community organizations.

Ms. White needs to be involved in the budget-making process, which occurs well before the fiscal year in which the funds are actually spent. She also needs to keep records showing uses made of library materials including notes about where the collection failed to meet needs and requests.

When Ms. White can show the administrators evidence and justification for her spending requests during the budget-making process, adjustments can be made. This process will need to be started a full year prior to her meeting with the administrators since the budget planning process for administrators occurs 6 months to a year before the actual spending occurs. *(MMJ)*

SPEND EVERY DIME

Ms. White has learned a good lesson. Always spend every dime in your budget. She also must plan her budget more carefully to reflect the real needs of the library media center. She must never let the budget become a static or automatic "always done that way" item. Good managers recognize the budget as the number-one tool for the program.

The state requirements may be cumbersome, but they do not create restrictions that can't be managed. *(JM)*

BIBLIOGRAPHY

American Association of School Librarians and Association for Educational Communications and Technology. *Information Power: Guidelines for School Library Media Programs.* Chicago: American Library Association, 1988.
See pages 49–51, 124–30. "At the building level, the head of the library

media program develops the individual school's library media budget, in cooperation with the principal and the district program director."

Buckingham, Betty Jo. "Planning the School Library Media Center Budget." Iowa State Department of Education, 1984. ERIC document ED 242 324.

Presents a plan for developing both long-range and short-range budgets based on specific goals and objectives. A sample budget is provided along with typical financial subaccount codes found in school systems.

Gillespie, John T., and Diana L. Spirt. *Administrating the School Library Media Center*. New York: R. R. Bowker, 1983.

See Chapter 4 on "Budget" for an excellent review of "accounting codes," "budget calendar," and "cost-allocation methods." Several budgeting systems are also clearly explained, including "lump-sum budget," "line-item budget," and "object expenditure."

Case 29: Facility Plan Gone Awry

Joe Lamont was excited as he approached Westside High School. The media center had been remodeled during the summer break, and he looked forward to the improvements in services the new facility would allow. Lamont had spent the last 8 weeks as a counselor in a wilderness camp in Colorado. Now he was back and ready to start his tenth year as school media specialist.

He had talked long and hard about the new facility with the principal. Over the past years, he had developed a strong service-oriented program within very cramped quarters. His program would "soar" in the new space.

As he entered the media center, Mr. Lamont could not believe his eyes. Who had planned this? Nothing was like the last blueprint he had seen. There was less than half as much space as he had been promised. The added shelving blocked the view of the leisure reading area. The computers were squeezed into individual work spaces next to the reference collection. The walls were painted orange, the new carpet was a light blue, and the tabletops were finished with a white formica. It looked like a circus to Mr. Lamont, not at all a study atmosphere. The new teacher workroom was not included. That space was now a storage room for old textbooks. The five new electrical outlets he had requested had been placed in that room, but were of no use if production of materials was now to be eliminated in favor of book storage. He could not find any of the additional outlets he had requested in the main library area. In fact, there was no place to plug in the computers regardless of where they might be placed in the library.

What had gone wrong? Mr. Lamont had been included in the early planning stages. He had met with the architect and the administration last winter. He had given his suggestions, had described the activities and services of the media center, and had even sketched a scale drawing that incorporated his ideas. Mr. Lamont had listed his specifications for equipment and for furniture. What did he forget? He knew that in other remodeling plans the school board had accepted "bargains" and substitutes for items requested. He knew there had been talk about the need for more storage space for the school's materials in general. Joe thought his facility plans were firmly set 3 months ago.

Consider the following:

a. What approach should Mr. Lamont take at this point?
b. Could Mr. Lamont have prevented any of the changes in plans?
c. Is there a way to undo the damage?
d. What are the roles of the media specialist, the principal, the school board, and the architect in the planning of facility design, either new or remodeled?

Response

EVERYONE HAS A ROLE AND A RESPONSIBILITY

The first thing Mr. Lamont needs to do is to be sure he has his anger under control. Then he needs to discover why the cuts and changes were made and what the administrators see as possibilities for amelioration in the future. He may wish to explore whether the architects followed the final guidelines they received. If they did not, the school may be able to seek some compensation or accommodation. It seems likely, however, that past signals should have warned Mr. Lamont about the board's penchant for compromise.

Soon after the public and the school board or the professional staff recognizes it needs to build or remodel a facility, consultants should be called in to help develop and/or revise educational specifications. Then an architect is selected by the board and superintendent. The board, the staff, and the architect should work together to develop, prepare, and revise schematic designs and preliminary building specifications. Then working drawings and building and equipment specifications should be prepared, revised, and approved, all with the involvement of the same three groups.

Actual monitoring of construction is the responsibility of the architect and the school board. But if Mr. Lamont had been present during the building process, he may have been able to flag some of the problems so the board could have kept a better handle on things. After remodeling, the board has to formally accept the completion of the task. After the acceptance, the architect is off the hook.

Actually the architect can have considerable control over how the facility is arranged, at least until after the acceptance and the open house. When the open house is over, Mr. Lamont can begin planning to rearrange the available space for best possible service. *(BJB)*

CORRECTING SOME OF THE PROBLEMS

There is probably no way, at least in the immediate future, that Mr. Lamont is going to regain the amount of space for which he hoped, but there are several things that he can do. He can work to persuade the district to discard the old textbooks, thus freeing the storeroom for whatever the highest priority was, production, computers, or faculty lesson planning.

Since Mr. Lamont did sketches for an expanded center, maybe he could try some sketches for how to use a small space better. For assistance in such planning he could turn to members of the library media consultant staff or the state department of education. They are usually very experienced at helping schools get the most out of inadequate facilities. There is probably some arrangement of furniture and shelving that would keep the stacks from blocking leisure reading space, for example.

The school district maintenance staff could add power poles or strips of outlets near the computers. With silencing covers for printers, and perhaps with earphones for "sound" computer programs, computers in the reading-listening-viewing room would be less distracting.

Since Mr. Lamont may need to live with orange walls for awhile, he may want to work with the art staff to cover the walls with murals or to use the walls for display of student art.

If the white formica tabletops have a dull finish, they would probably not cause eye strain. However, if glare is a problem, Mr. Lamont could cover the tops of the tables with a dull surfaced contact paper. This is not a permanent solution. The contact paper would have to be replaced from time to time. *(BJB)*

THE EDUCATOR'S ROLE

The roles of the principal and the media specialist are limited but can be influential. They should be very much involved in developing the educational philosophy of the school and of the library media center, consulting with specialists and preparing educational specifications. The principal should work to see that the staff members have an opportunity to work with the architect. The library media specialist should define what will happen in the media center, how many different things will be happening at the same time, and what the traffic flow will be. The library media specialist should know how much of what kind of shelving, storage, seating, and work space is needed, and should be able to give an estimate of the total space needed. However, the final decision on space is not the right or responsibility of the library media specialist, and so contingency plans are necessary to save as much of the program as possible if the space is cut or changed. *(BJB)*

THE ARCHITECT'S ROLE

The school board and its executive officer, the superintendent, acquire the site; agree to provide for enlargements, additions, or new facilities; propose levies to pay for the building and fixtures; initiate studies to determine need; approve educational specifications; and employ an architect. With the assistance of the architect they approve the preliminary and final drawings, seek bonding support, conduct the bidding, and oversee the construction. They also accept completion of the project.

The architect provides schematic designs and preliminary building specifications, consults with specialists and faculty, prepares working drawings and final building and equipment specifications, prepares the budget, assists the board with bonding and bidding, and oversees the construction. The architect has a large degree of control from the time of approval of the final specifications until the board accepts the facility.

After the facility is accepted, the principal and the library media specialist are responsible for its use and adaptation. *(BJB)*

REVISIONS WILL OFTEN BE MADE

Mr. Lamont is in a real dilemma with a high expectation level and facilities that he perceives will hamper his service to teachers and students. After 10 years of experience one may have expected Mr. Lamont to have given more attention to the need for following through with plans. There is little or nothing that Mr. Lamont can do at this time. He is apparently a flexible person with a history of coping with less-than-desirable environments, but options are almost nonexistent. Mr. Lamont's major mistake was his assumption that the decision makers would follow his plan even though he chose to make himself unavailable during the critical negotiation period which all school building programs encounter in the final design and building process. His behavior is even more puzzling because he was aware that the board had set precedents for compromising quality for "bargains." Surely Mr. Lamont knew blueprints undergo numerous revisions. One must wonder whether Mr. Lamont is not the victim of his own behaviors and naivete.

The media specialist has the responsibility to educate administrators, board members, and architects about the appropriate use of space, safety standards, special needs for disabled persons, customary services, and the need for flexibility of space to accommodate state-of-the-art technologies as they become available. Administrators have the responsibility to involve the librarian and/or consultants at all decision-making levels and to recognize the economy of purchasing quality equipment and materials. Architects need to be aware of the function of the media center and solicit ideas from those who work in that environment. Functional media centers must be aesthetically pleasing, but aesthetics and function are not mutually exclusive. *(AH)*

BIBLIOGRAPHY

American Association of School Librarians and Association for Educational Communications and Technology. *Information Power: Guidelines for School Library Media Programs.* Chicago: American Library Association, 1988.
See pages 85–101. "When a decision is made to remodel a present facility or construct a new building or library media center, the library staff should take part from the beginning in all aspects of the planning."

Bedenbaugh, Edna. "Facility Planning in the School Media Center." *Indiana Media Journal* 9(4) (1987): 3–4.
A listing of important items to keep in mind during the facility planning process.

Butler, Naomi, and Yale Stenzler. "The Planning and Modification of Library Media Centers." *Drexel Library Quarterly* 13(2) (1977): 62–79.
Although a little dated, this article covers many of the important principles for planning media facilities. Emphasis is placed on the relationship of various function areas.

Lamkin, Bernice. "A Media Center for the 21st Century." *School Library Journal* 33(3) (1986): 25–29.
A planning process for a modern facility in a high school learning environment.

Library Learning Resources Facilities: New and Remodeled. Austin, TX: Texas Education Agency, 1982.
Provides a large variety of sample floor plans for school library media centers. An excellent guide to gathering essential information necessary to summarize the facility plan and specifications.

Patrick, Retta. *Facilities for School Library Media Centers: A Guide for Designing and Remodeling.* Littleton, CO: Libraries Unlimited, in press 1989.
On the basis of her experiences as a progressive media district supervisor, Patrick gives much insight into the planning of workable facilities and the cooperative input needed by all parties involved.

Prostano, Emanuel T., and Joyce S. Prostano. *The School Library Media Center.* Littleton, CO: Libraries Unlimited, 1987.
Chapter 6, "Facilities and Furniture," has one of the few outlines available for the media specialist who wants to design a new facility or remodel a current one. Roles of the many participants in the design process are defined.

Rockwood, Persis Emmett, and Christine Koontz Lynch. "Media Center Layout: A Marketing-Based Plan." In *School Library Media Annual.* Vol. 4, pp. 297–306. Littleton, CO: Libraries Unlimited, 1986.
This is excellent reading for the school media specialist who wants to redesign the current media center, keeping in mind the traffic patterns of the patrons.

Seager, Donald E. "Planning and Designing Media Facilities." *American School and University* (1977–78).
Presents a series of short articles with many helpful hints to today's media specialist even though the articles are a little dated now. "The Don't and the Do's" (September 1977): 20–21; "Let's Consider Space" (February 1978): 50–51; "Let's Talk Space to Space" (April 1978): 30–31; "Let's Get Specific" (June 1978): 50–51; "Let's Furnish" (August 1978): 48–49; "Let's Lock Up" (October 1978): 58–59; and "Let's Look at the Big Picture" (December 1978): 28–29.

Case 30: Finding Federal Funds

Discussion ──────────────────────────────────

Ann Balsam had an undergraduate degree from the small liberal arts college in her hometown and certification as a school media specialist. She taught second grade for 2 years and then took the library media position which opened 3 years ago at Lone Pine Elementary, only 20 miles from her college. Ms. Balsam had continued her education by entering into a graduate program in information science at the university. She had completed nine credit hours over the past two summers.

One class she had completed last summer was a special seminar in the management of district media programs. The class session on budgeting was team-taught by her professor and a consultant from the state's department of public instruction. Ms. Balsam was surprised to learn that all schools in the state were allocated federal funds and that block grant moneys were spent largely on library materials and equipment. Her school district did not receive this money, she insisted. She had never received any, at least to her knowledge. The state consultant showed Ms. Balsam a chart with the division of the funding last year, and her school district received over $29,000.

The consultant discussed the federal regulation which required that a committee of teachers and parents, as well as administrators, develop the plan concerning local use of the funds. Although other special instructional areas could also use the moneys, media services were often a target area. Ms. Balsam began to wonder what her school district had decided over the past years, and if any media professionals had been involved in the planning. "Media specialists are not *required* to be on the committee," stated the consultant. "It is up to the local media specialist to seek out this committee if he or she has not been notified by the administration. In most school districts, however, media specialists have taken a leading voice in the planning for the use of these funds."

Consider the following:

a. What steps should Ms. Balsam take to find out how federal funds are spent in her school system?
b. Should school districts be required to share financial information with the media staff?
c. What methods might encourage greater participation in the decision-making process concerning local use of federal money?
d. Once Ms. Balsam has the information concerning the block grant program, how should she approach the administration with her ideas on use of the money?

Response

WORK WITH THE ADMINISTRATION

Ms. Balsam's first step should be to discuss the matter with her building principal. Her approach would be to inform the principal of the knowledge she has gained through her class and to ask how the funds are allocated in the school district. Her principal should be able to provide her with the information, provided he or she has this knowledge. If funds are being used in the building, she might indicate an interest in serving on the committee that is making these decisions. *(GH)*

TALK TO THE CENTRAL OFFICE

Should the principal not be able to answer Ms. Balsam's questions, she should request permission to contact the individual in the central administrative office who is in charge of federal grants, if not the superintendent. One approach would be to indicate an interest in the program and volunteer to serve on the committee that determines how the funds are allocated. By informing the committee of what she had learned, and by indicating an interest, she may have a better opportunity to help to bring about changes and to see that some of the funds are allocated for the media centers than if she approaches the situation in a negative manner. *(GH)*

WORK WITH TEACHERS

A good media person is able to find those staff members who have projects they would like to have funded. By working together and including the principal in the project planning, the staff members become aware of the federal regulations regarding grant applications.

As the staff become aware of these funds, they will provide the additional support that is needed to have an effect on how funds are allocated. This is also a good way to promote library/media programs as an integral part of the curriculum. *(JM)*

WRITE A PROGRAM PROPOSAL

Any media specialist should consider writing a program proposal. Goals to be reached, the way funds would be spent, the way students and staff would benefit, and the number of people who would be affected by this new program should be part of the proposal. Submit this to the designated committee or group who decides on the approval of federally funded programs. Since the media specialist has worked with teachers, involve the teachers in the writing for best results. *(GH)*

COMMUNICATION IS AN ANSWER

Ms. Balsam has not been aware of the sources of funding, in particular the federal block grant money received by her district. She needs to communicate with those in the district to find out how the funds have been spent. *(GH)*

ENCOURAGE GREATER PARTICIPATION IN THE DECISION-MAKING PROCESS

1. Recruitment for committee membership should be done openly.
2. Those whose programs are involved should be represented.
3. Committee decisions and reports should be made available.

Ann should approach the administration with her ideas by doing the following:

1. Write clear, justifiable, and accountable goals.
2. Garner support for these goals:
   a. Horizontally through her peers (other media specialists, teachers) to present a unified position.
   b. Vertically through her building administrator and district media supervisor.
   c. Through student, parent, and community support.
3. Get membership on or influence with the committee.
   a. Realize it's a political entity of special interests, especially science education, vocational education, and special education.
   b. Investigate the members and find the power base. *(KC)*

GATHER INFORMATION ON HOW FUNDING HAS BEEN SPENT

Initially, the library media specialist might want to do some background work before discussing the problems with the administration.

1. Visit the school district's business office to look at records of money spent for library materials in the past several years. Were federal funds spent for library material in the past? If they were, why does the library media center no longer receive the money?
2. Contact library media specialists from other schools in the area to find out if they receive federal funds. If they do, how did they go about getting the funds?
3. If there is a state school library media specialist that works with the school systems, this person might want to be contacted for information and advice.
4. The library media specialist should do some research into federal funding and become knowledgeable about what funds are available and how they are allocated. From this research she would find that most libraries receive their funds from the Block Grant Consolidation, the old ESEA IV-B, which is the only federal education program with funds for school libraries.

The next step to the solution of this problem might be for the library media specialist to discuss with the principal or appropriate administrator the possibility of being included on the committee that develops the plan for local use of the funds.

There is the possibility that even when the library media specialist asks to be on the committee that plans for the spending of federal funds, she will be denied the request. And if she does get on the committee, there is no guarantee that the group will agree to allocate any of the money to the library.

Thus the wise library media specialist will attempt to gain informal power in the absence of formal power. One of the best ways to gain informal power is through communication. Frequency and quality of communication are basic factors in the program survival of any library media center.

With these things in mind, the library media specialist should do some communication planning. She should, whenever possible, let the administration and teachers know of successes and needs in the library. This promotion and justification of the library media center could "remind" the administration that the library media center could spend federal funding in such a way that the entire curriculum benefits. *(JT)*

A school district's financial records are open to the public. Ms. Balsam should be able to find out how Chapter 2 funding is spent. She will also find that the block grant does not have to be spent for library media resources. The federal legislation clearly leaves the decision on what projects to fund to the school. If she wants to participate, Ms. Balsam must communicate her interest. She should go to her principal with a project that reflects a documented need and a purpose that will benefit the students. *(JM)*

BIBLIOGRAPHY

Cole, Georgia. "ECIA Chapter 2 in Indiana Schools." *Indiana Media Journal* 7(4) (1985): 23–32.
This is a detailed report of how one state allocates the block grant funds.

Gerhardt, Lillian N. "Talking about ESEA." *School Library Journal* 32(4) (1985): 2.
Gerhardt reviews the impact of ESEA on the development of school library programs and the effect on publication of books for young adults.

Miller, Marilyn Lea. "Statement before the Subcommittee of Education, Arts, and Humanities, Senate Labor and Human Resources Committee on Reauthorization of Chapter 2, Education Consolidation and School Improvement Act, July 16, 1987." *School Library Media Quarterly* 16(2) (1988): 122–26.
A justification of the merits of school programs and the need for continued support from the government as given by one of the leaders of the Association of American School Librarians.

Pattie, Kenton, and Mary Ernst. "Chapter 11 Grants: Libraries Gain." *School Library Journal* 29(5) (1983): 17–20.
This article describes the shift in federal funds from categorical to block grants. It also describes how several large school districts allocate such federal money and concludes that much of the federal money would probably be invested in microcomputer systems. This prediction, of course, was on target, as well over 65% of the federal dollars have been invested in computer-related equipment and activities since 1985.

Case 31: Selling Interlibrary Loan

Description

Kathy Winner has just returned from the national conference of the American Association of School Librarians. In many presentations, and as she talked with other senior high school librarians, the excitement seemed to center on new databases available on CD-ROM and the potential for young adults to experience the "information age." Ms. Winner returned to her school ready to approach teachers and her principal with the news.

Ms. Winner finds, however, that barriers to establishing the electronic information center are many. Most teachers are doubtful that the additional sources the students might locate through the use of online searching or the CD-ROM databases will actually be used. "Sources currently held in the library are enough for my students, and I don't want to wait for materials to be sent from some other school or library." "My students seldom use the card catalog and the *Reader's Guide*, so why bring all of this other stuff in?"

Not only did Ms. Winner receive little support for expanding the information possibilities for the students, but many of the teachers seemed not to even understand the manner in which citations were stored and retrieved through these new electronic formats. "We would need to take time to learn how to search, and I don't have the time." "I don't care where my kids get their 10 sources for their paper, as long as they get 10 sources....I never judge the quality of the materials they select anyway."

When Ms. Winner's principal learns the price tag of the CD-ROM services, he concludes that this is all too costly for the library program. "To invest in one CD-ROM database along with the terminal and printer would cost us nearly as much as you currently have budgeted for the entire media center program." In addition, the principal doubts that the students would make serious use of the materials obtained through interlibrary loan. "What do they need all of these magazines for anyway?"

Ms. Winner's principal later informs her that he has learned that a neighboring school district has joined a network of libraries and will plan to share materials with public libraries and college libraries. "It's going to cost them," he tells Ms. Winner, "and I can't see that they have anything a college library would want to borrow. Besides, we would never let our instructional materials be loaned to community groups or to any other library. We need those things here, ready for our teachers to use when they are needed, and available on short notice."

As Ms. Winner:

a. How would you attempt to get teachers involved in the potential for using databases available on CD-ROM, including ERIC, NewsBank, InfoTrack, Wilsondisc, and others?
b. How do you demonstrate the value of the school district becoming a member of a resource-sharing network? Is it reasonable to expect teachers to allow "their" instructional materials to be loaned beyond the local school?
c. What issues need to be addressed in a long-range plan for the development and implementation of a "modern electronic information age" school library media program?

Response

CONSIDER ALL POTENTIAL COSTS

The potential for the secondary school in the use of CD-ROM databases is truly exciting. In several pilot projects over the past 10 years, it has been demonstrated over and over again that young people can search successfully for information and will make wise choices in the request for materials through interlibrary loan. It provides the groundwork for the information challenges that will follow these students in their college and professional years. The initial cost for such systems, however, may be very substantial. Not since the late 1960s when television studios were established in many school corporations has there been a need for a commitment of such large amounts of capital.

Ms. Winner should probably start with a few teachers at a time. She can demonstrate the potential by taking them to the local college library and showing them how various searches take place and what kind of information can be identified over and above that contained in the school library. Together, Kathy and the teachers can examine questions such as: What can access to more information do to increase the demands placed on the students as they write their term papers? How can the teacher and the library media specialist begin to work together to help the student make wise selections of the best materials to use from the growing field of information? What new topic areas for term papers become "doable" now that access to the information is possible? As Ms. Winner begins to work with a few teachers to reach answers to these questions, she will find that several will become very supportive of trying to acquire such databases for the school.

Of course, the expense of CD-ROM systems does not stop at just the software and the hardware. Ms. Winner will need also to find ways to demonstrate that there is value in sharing resources. She will need to bring to the attention of teachers and administrators the fact that resource sharing may result in some items not being as immediately available as before, but that because materials beyond the school's collection will be available as never before, the trade-off will be well worth the possible minor inconveniences.

In her long-range planning, Ms. Winner will need to be sure that she does not fall short in the estimates for complete expenses. Too many television studios were built 20 years ago with just enough money for equipment and no money for maintaining equipment, support staff, inservice education for teachers, and community involvement. Most of those studios are no longer functional. The same may become true in the development of expanded information systems in secondary schools. Often money will be found immediately for equipment when the administration has been convinced of the need. However, for the electronic information age to become an effective part of secondary school public education, money must be available for postage and shipping expenses, training of library staff and teaching staff, and the purchase of additional materials (periodicals or microfilm) necessary to support the database.

Finally, Ms. Winner will need to devote some time not only to training teachers in the use of databases, but to convincing teachers that they will need to be ready to assist their students in learning how to use these electronic systems. School media specialists who already have their electronic database systems up and running are often willing to come and help with such training. Ms. Winner may want to contact a regional or central office of her state library system, as most now have a staff of consultants who are willing to come and provide workshops in the use of databases and interlibrary loan.

In addition, Ms. Winner will need to develop workshops dealing with information selection and information use. This will be the most difficult part of the development of the entire program, as teachers will resist the additional time which must be given to a student to complete a term paper that includes getting materials through interlibrary loan, and the additional time and expertise necessary to evaluate a student's paper on the quality as well as the quantity of sources used. *(DC)*

BIBLIOGRAPHY

American Association of School Librarians and Association for Educational Communications and Technology. *Information Power: Guidelines for School Library Media Programs.* Chicago: American Library Association, 1988.
See pages 1–13, 81–83. "Challenge: To participate in networks that enhance access to resources located outside the school."

Aversa, Elizabeth S., and Jacqueline C. Mancall. *Management of Online Search Services in Schools.* Santa Barbara, CA: ABC-CLIO, 1989.
Although there are more examples of forms and methods for documentation given in the guide than most school library media specialists will ever want to use, this is the best and most current book available to give direction in the marketing and justification of online and interlibrary loan services in public schools.

Callison, Daniel, "Methods for Measuring Student Use of Databases and Interlibrary Loan Materials." *School Library Media Quarterly* 16(2) (1988): 138–42.
High school students used over 70% of the books obtained though interlibrary loan and just over 30% of the journal articles obtained.

Callison, Daniel, and Ann Daniels. "Introducing End-User Software for Enhancing Student Online Searching." *School Library Media Quarterly* 16(3) (1988): 173–81.
Forms are given for helping students narrow the topic and identify terms for searching on Wilsonline. Characteristics of successful student searchers are listed (those who planned ahead and had time to revise searches after their first interlibrary loan requests were received tended to be more successful in locating useful materials).

———. "Using Wilsearch with High School Students: A Pilot Study." Indiana University, ERIC Document Reproduction Service, 1986. ERIC document 275 343.
Presents a full technical report on the student use of interlibrary loan and the extent of student use of each electronic database offered by Wilsonline. Also outlined is an extended timeline for the typical high school term paper assignment which allows for more time for the students to receive items through interlibrary loan, to review those materials, and to seek leads to more materials before concluding the paper.

Craver, Kathleen W. "Teaching Online Bibliographic Searching to High School Students." *Top of the News* 41(2) (1985): 131–38.
This project involved the use of Dialog and student access to over 50 different databases.

———. "The Influence of Online Catalogs on Academic Library Use by College-Bound High School Seniors." *RQ* 28(2) (1988): 220–31.
The results of this study confirm the positive influence the availability of an academic online catalog in a school library has on the use of academic libraries by college-bound high school seniors. Analysis of the data revealed that students who had access to an academic online catalog at University High School Library cited more materials from the University

of Illinois Library than students who did not have access to a school library online catalog.

Mancall, Jacqueline C., and Dreama Deskins. "High School Students, Librarians, and the Search Process." ERIC Document Reproduction Service, 1986. ERIC document 262 823.

Few of the references that came up online were used by students in their bibliographies. This may have been due to the fact that materials retrieved online either were too sophisticated for the student to consider or were impossible to locate.

Pruitt, Ellen, and Karen Dowling. "Searching for Current Information Online." *Online* 9(2) (1985): 47–60.

This project demonstrated the need for increasing the timeline for the student assignment. The use of interlibrary loaned materials requires a wait of two to four weeks.

School Library Media Quarterly 16(2) (1988).

This issue has several articles which will help and encourage the school media specialist who wants to plan an inservice training program for teachers. Training in online searching and use of other new information technologies is ranked high in a needs assessment on continuing education. These data are reported by Jacqueline C. Mancall and Linda H. Bertland. Articles of interest include "Role of Professional Development Activities in Promoting Improved Instructional Services in the Library Media Program," by Shirley L. Aaron; "Understanding and Facilitating Adult Learning," by Stephen D. Brookfield; "In-Service and the School Library Media Specialist: What Works and What Doesn't," by Philip M. Turner; and "Library Media Specialists in a Staff Development Role," by J. Foster Watkins and Anne Hale Craft.

Tenopir, Carol. "Online Databases: Online Searching in Schools." *Library Journal* 111(2): (1986): 60–61.

Outlines the potential market for popular databases in the public school and the way distributors are moving to develop that market.

Walker, H. Thomas. "Networking and School Library Media Centers." *School Library Media Quarterly* 12(1): (1983): 20–28.

Walker reports that students were highly selective and serious about identification of materials that might be borrowed from some other library.

Wozny, Lucy Anne. "Online Bibliographic Searching and Student Use of Information." *School Library Media Quarterly* 11(1) (1981): 35–42.

Online searching played a key role in the teacher's and librarian's objective to make the students aware of the diversity of institutions that supply information, as the process allowed them to identify new sources and recommend information centers beyond the students' own school library.

Case 32: Helping the Disabled

Description

Dodge Senior High School was constructed in 1932. It was the first high school in the nation to cost $1 million to complete, and it was a model facility for decades in the Midwest. Fine craftsmanship was displayed in the carpentry and other details of the building's design. Such craftsmanship was no longer expected in public schools, but during the Depression years such care could be given because labor—even highly skilled labor—was cheap. Although the structure was beautiful, with a 150-foot-high tower dominating the grounds, the three-story building was not constructed with the physically disabled in mind.

Over 50 years after the completion of the building and well past the time federal legislation was passed to require equal access to educational facilities for all students regardless of mental or physical disabilities, Dan Cranston found that the media center facility he managed at DHS had many barriers to open access to materials for those who could not climb stairs. The periodical collection, for example, was located in a balcony area. Two students who attend the school are in wheelchairs. Not only was the balcony area inaccessible for them, but doorways to small rooms adjoining the main reading area were too small for either wheelchair to enter. Thus, the collections that included the sciences, history, and biographies were beyond the reach of these two students.

It was obvious not only that something had to be done to make the materials more accessible for not only the disabled students mentioned above, but that there needed to be an evaluation of the entire facility with the goal of providing full service to disabled students.

As Mr. Cranston:

   a. What are some suggestions you would make for meeting the needs of the two students in wheelchairs?

b. What other potential barriers should be looked for that may cause problems for other students who might be physically disadvantaged?

c. To what extent does an individual school have the responsibility to serve the needs of the disabled minority, especially when such special services require additional investment of time and money?

Response

Mr. Cranston should give a great deal of time and attention to serving those students who may have a physical or mental disability. It may be that the changes in the facility cannot be made immediately, but certainly student assistants can be used to retrieve materials for the two physically disabled students. It may even mean that a student assistant will need to be assigned to these students so that the student assistant gets to know the reading tastes and information needs to the degree that he or she can actually browse the shelves for the disabled student in the areas that are not accessible.

Such service, even if it could develop to such a fine relationship, should not be a substitute for opening the facility to all students. It may be costly, but the school should invest in allowing access to all areas of the collection, even if this means reconstructing expensive doorways. In the case of the periodical collection being housed in a balcony area, perhaps it could be made accessible if a doorway were made from the balcony to the hallway on the floor above the library. Then the balcony area would be accessible, assuming an elevator would take the students to the higher floor, and from there they could enter the periodicals area on their own.

New media center facilities should always be designed with open access to *all* areas for all students. Mainstreaming involves more than use of the classroom and the instructional delivery of the teacher. Mainstreaming must also include the full services offered by the school library media program. *(DC)*

BIBLIOGRAPHY

American Association of School Librarians and Association for Educational Communications and Technology. *Information Power: Guidelines for School Library Media Programs.* Chicago: American Library Association, 1988.
See pages 89–96. "...providing barrier-free routes for physically impaired patrons, with particular attention to bookstack areas, catalog and circulation areas, and seating spaces."

Baskin, Barbara H., and Karen H. Harris, eds. *The Mainstreamed Library: Issues, Ideas, Innovations.* Chicago: American Library Association, 1982.
Of special interest are these chapters: "Users Come First in Design," by Philip M. Bennett; "An Examination of Physical and Attitudinal Barriers to Handicapped Library Users," by Robert T. Begg; and "Design Criteria for Educational Facilities for Special Education Services," by Allen C. Abend.

Library Learning Resources Facilities: New and Remodeled. Austin, TX: Texas Education Agency, 1982.
Lists specific requirements for "accessibility by the handicapped," under Section 504 of the Rehabilitation Act of 1973.

Lucas, Linda, and Marilyn H. Karrenbrock. *The Disabled Child in the Library.* Littleton, CO: Libraries Unlimited, 1983.
Although this excellent publication has important information throughout, the relevant chapter to this case is chapter 9, "Creating Mainstreamed Environments." Legislation and standards, basic rules for good facility design, selection of furnishings, lighting, and climate control, as well as special problems for children with mobility and dexterity disabilities, are covered.

Index

Compiled by Debbie Burnham-Kidwell